THE FUTURE OF CLOTHING

BLOOMSBURY VISUAL ARTS
Bloomsbury Publishing Plc
50 Bedford Square, London, WC1B 3DP, UK
1385 Broadway, New York, NY 10018, USA
29 Earlsfort Terrace, Dublin 2, Ireland

First published in Great Britain 2023

Cover design: W.I.R.E
Cover image © Jonathan Bartlett

A catalogue record for this book is available from the British Library.

Library of Congress Cataloging-in-Publication Data
Names: Achermann, Simone, author. | Sigrist, Stephan, author.
Title: The future of clothing : will we wear suits on Mars? /
Simone Achermann and Stephan Sigrist.
Description: London ; New York : Bloomsbury Visual Arts, 2022. |
Includes bibliographical references and index.
Identifiers: LCCN 2021042784 (print) | LCCN 2021042785 (ebook) |
ISBN 9781350138599 (hardback) | ISBN 9781350138605 (ebook) |
ISBN 9781350138612 (pdf)
Subjects: LCSH: Clothing trade–Forecasting. | Fashion–Forecasting.
Classification: LCC TT497 .A25 2022 (print) | LCC TT497 (ebook) | DDC
746.9/2–dc23
LC record available at https://lccn.loc.gov/2021042784
LC ebook record available at https://lccn.loc.gov/2021042785

ISBN: HB: 978-1-3501-3859-9
ePDF: 978-1-3501-3861-2
eBook: 978-1-3501-3860-5

Typeset by W.I.R.E. and Integra Software Services Pvt. Ltd.
Printed and bound in India

THE FUTURE OF CLOTHING

WILL WE WEAR SUITS ON MARS?

SIMONE ACHERMANN AND
STEPHAN SIGRIST

BLOOMSBURY VISUAL ARTS
LONDON • NEW YORK • OXFORD • NEW DELHI • SYDNEY

PREFACE

WILL WE WEAR BESPOKE SUITS ON MARS?

As Scabal approaches its 85th birthday, we wanted to take a moment to reflect not just on our history but perhaps more importantly on what the future could hold for us and our industry as a whole.

Looking forward has always been part of our DNA. Even though we sincerely value all the heritage and experience we have built up over the years – the leaders of this company have always found time to pause and think about the next step. Our founder Otto Hertz, his successor Peter Thissen (my father) and I have always been very keen to take a look not only into our own future but also the future of all that surrounds us. Partly out of interest and intellectual challenge but obviously also to make sure that as a brand we always remain relevant and in a position to successfully face, and sometimes anticipate, upcoming changes.

This thought process has long been in our history, and led us in 1971 to a collaboration with Salvador Dali. The world-famous artist and dandy was asked to create his own vision of what fashion could look like in the year 2000. Dali took inspiration from 12 classical masterpieces from the Louvre collection and reinterpreted them in his very own surrealist way to

Salvador Dalí and Otto Hertz, the founder of Scabal, 1972.

paint a mind-boggling picture of what he thought fashion would become. Whether he was right or wrong is difficult to say – he certainly got a few things right – but more importantly his work raised questions, provoked ideas and made us and others think twice about what was to come.

Today our company values are very clear to us and they guide us in everything we undertake in the present and give us a framework for our future plans. We strongly believe in respect, respect for all people, but also respect for the environment. Sustainability of our products and through our whole enterprise is an important aspect of what we do and who we are.

As a luxury cloth merchant who caters to the bespoke offerings of the world's leading tailors and brands and within our own sartorial tailoring collections, we also believe in the expression of individuality. It is the elegance of the style of clothing and the elegance of the mind behind the individual wearer that inspires us every day.

"The ages that looked the most avidly to their future, were those that recorded the passing of time with the most splendid modes."

SALVADOR DALI

The official unveiling of the Salvador Dalì for Scabal paintings at the Hotel Maurice in Paris, 1971.

As technologies pervade our worlds, we take confidence in the value of the human touch as a guarantor of quality, style and longevity. In our mind, crafted products, made in a transparent, traceable way according to the ancient ethos of quality are the foundations of true luxury.

These convictions have driven us for the last 80 years and we would love to see them perpetuated. But will they resist the test of time?

To answer this question, we have teamed up with Swiss think tank W.I.R.E., along with a collection of contributors whose pieces you will read throughout this book. We wanted to challenge our views and convictions and compare them to the views of thought leaders, historians, industry experts and visionaries. W.I.R.E. have a strong track record in challenging clichés, looking into the future in a non-conventional way and generally providing high-level thought-provoking publications.

Our contributors come from a very wide array of fields ranging from history to environmental activism and from fashion to the luxury industry, all sharing a wealth of expertise along with strong opinions. Their views combined with the theoretical research conducted by W.I.R.E. will provide the backdrop to a series of theses and scenarios of where our future might be leading us.

We also wanted to continue exploring how the art world interprets their vision of the future, so we have teamed up with one of the world's most prolific contemporary artists, John Armleder, and tasked him with creating a piece that illustrates his ideas for how the future will develop.

Of course, this book cannot have the ambition to give definitive answers to all the questions raised about the future, it is not a scientific study. Our overarching goal here is to make us all think critically about our own assumptions for the future and stir up some healthy debates.

We sincerely hope that you will take as much pleasure reflecting on the possibilities of these future scenarios as we have enjoyed working on them.

Happy reading and a happy future ...

Gregor Thissen
Executive Chairman
Scabal Group

INTRODUCTION

DRESS ME UP, SCOTTY!

Quindao, China, 12 am. Big black buses are cruising through the city, park themselves at busy places, open their doors, lower their silver stairs and wait for the first customers. People start flocking into the "Magic Bus". One after the other is positioning themselves in front of a light beam apparatus for a few seconds to be measured for a custom-made suit that will be sent to their homes some days later.

What seems to be the scene from a science fiction movie is the description of what a Chinese suit maker has started to offer a few years ago.[1] Will Commander Spock of the series "Star Trek" soon tell his suit to beam him up? Even if we look at less trailblazing examples, clothing seems to be on the brink of fundamental change. Again. Until the 19th century manufacturing of clothing was so labour intensive that most people could not afford it – which in most cases meant making their own garments or sharing good pants with relatives and wearing them until they fall apart. With the industrial revolution, much of the human work was replaced by machines; production standardised. Until today, there has been a steady process of increasing efficiency – from automated ironing to cutting room management software – which eventually led us to fast fashion. Now we can buy a shirt to wear it once.

Currently, we are expecting not only to reach a next level of efficiency, but another revolution in clothing, in terms of production and function. Regarding production, two aspects play a major role. One is the automation of the actual manufacturing of the finished garment, which is supposed to happen with the use of sewing robots. The other is the personalisation of fabrication with "mass-made-to-measure" – the cheap production of custom-made suits with the use of prefabricated blocks, which are then adapted to the individual's measurements. A further individualisation beyond measurements is aspired to with the development of AI-design programs that assist the customer in creating a garment before it is produced by an external supplier. Being able to produce individually and cheaply would mean no less than the end of the principles of the economy of scale, in which low price goods can only be achieved by the production of high quantities.

Regarding the function of clothing, the promises of the future are no less fundamental. Until today, clothes had two main purposes. First, to protect us from nature, such as cold, heat, wind and rain. And second, to represent status and belonging; that is to show our position in society, in private and working environments and to mark the community, culture, religion or gender we belong to or identify with. There are no signs that these traditional roles of clothing will be replaced, but that they could be lived and experienced in a different way. With the progress in material sciences, garments might soon not only shield us from cold and heat but also from future pandemics, as indicated by the recent development of protective everyday clothing, such as the virus-resistant Full Metal Jacket.[2] The fusion of electronics and fabric in smart clothing, moreover, will allow textiles not only to protect us from harm but to actively control our health – by monitoring our heartbeat, warn us of air pollution or detect early signs of cancer in our bodies.[3] In addition, functional clothes could play a vital role in navigating us through our increasingly intelligent environment. Until recently, the cell phone was considered the ideal tool to control the digital infrastructure. Today, it is clothes – as they are closer to our bodies, don't need to be carried around or get lost.

The role of expressing status and belonging also seems at the point of being re-defined. Fading hierarchies, blurring class identification and an increasingly heterogeneous, individualised society have already led to a continuous dressing down and the fading of traditional dress codes. What started with the casual Friday resulted in the triumph of streetwear. Also, the recent trend towards gender-neutral clothes – a famous example is the UK department store John Lewis' abolition of boys' and girls' departments – seems to be shaking the existing codex. The decision of what to wear and for which occasion is increasingly in the hands of the individuals and their peers – the logical consequence would be much more individuality expressed in clothing and new dress codes within the new communities – from environmentalists wearing highly sustainable clothes, to pioneers for gender-neutral clothing and the committed wearers of suit and tie.

CONTINUITY AND OLD IMAGES OF TOMORROW

At the same time, change seems slow. Many of the alleged breakthroughs are far from market entry. Until today, sewing machines are not nearly as precise as human hands; several suppliers of mass-made-to-measure and AI-designed clothes had to take their garments back as they were badly fitting; functional clothing already on the market, such as Google's and Levi's smart jacket Jacquard, are not crowned with success. And even though dress codes are less compulsory, people prefer not to stand out in the crowd. A walk through the city shows: Little of that radical change on the horizon can be felt. Casualisation of clothing did not lead to more individuality, but more sameness: jeans and shirt for all. And even if mass-made-to-measure hits the high street, if everyone has it, it is no longer personalised. Moreover, many seemingly new developments, like gender-neutral garments, are actually not as new as we might think; the differentiation between boys' and girls' clothes is a relatively recent invention.

One reason for this consistency could be the simple fact that clothing is a basic need: Clothes, most of all, need to fit us, be comfortable and look decent. This might also explain why clothing – as well as food – has rarely been the main topic for visionaries. In film, even in the sci-fi genre, there is hardly any breakthrough imagery of future clothing to be found. And the few exceptions, such as the outfits represented in the space age movies of the 1960s, have been re-used over the years.

Does this mean the revolution is already behind us and we won't witness the kind of change our forebears did in the 19th century? Time to have a close and critical look at the recent developments in clothing and their possible consequences for the future: from the development of new manmade materials, the strive for more sustainability, the attempts to fuse electronic components with textiles, fading dress codes, the gender-neutral movement, visualisation of design and the democratisation of production. (⟼ Chapter I, p. 1)

However, the question is not only how much change will happen and which elements might remain the same or how many of the new products, trends and fabrication methods will have market potential. We also have to ask ourselves what should be changed – so that the quality of clothing is guaranteed and the individuals and society as a whole can profit. Much of the discourse on the future of clothing is centred on new technologies. Yet the current changes are more far-reaching and affect not only clothing itself but also the way we interact, communicate and express status. They will also affect the business of other fields, with which clothing will become increasingly interconnected.

Let us assume clothes will be able to control various aspects of our health on a daily basis. This will not only potentially make us healthier, but also increase our dependency on technology, alter – or dictate – our lifestyle, and rearrange the business landscape: providers of clothing will need to cooperate with providers of electronics and healthcare and, depending on the degree of functionalization of the product, might even be replaced by them. Also, if we succeed in fully automating the production of clothing, this will not only have an impact on the affordability of clothes, but also on the role of the human work in fabricating them, our attempts to reduce waste and make the industry more sustainable as well as the future of the thousands of employees in low wage countries. Moreover, a breakthrough in the cheap production of made-to-measure clothing will change the value of handmade clothing, the way we define luxury and it will question the possibility of individualisation in times of mass-individualisation. At the same time, developments outside fashion will also change clothing: If a majority of future fashion models are avatars and assistive robots become part of our families, the design of clothing will necessarily change – as will the wearers.

With these interconnections in mind, the purpose of this book is not only to discuss the future of clothing but also to widen the discourse with a trans-disciplinary approach. What will luxury mean tomorrow? How important is human work for the clothing industry? How does AI design affect individualisation? What happens to craftsmanship in times of automation? What are the consequences of mass-made-to-measure for bespoke tailoring? Will new man-made materials make the industry more sustainable? What are clothes capable and incapable of doing for us tomorrow – and what does that mean for us? How new are the current changes? And: What will the future wearers look like?

Academics, entrepreneurs and makers from the area of clothing and beyond are talking about the latest developments and share their ideas and opinions on the future of clothing. (⟼ Chapter II, p. 33). This book will mainly engage with the following subthemes: sustainability, luxury, craftsmanship, gender, individualisation, functionalization as well as change and continuity in general. Fashion historian Amber Butchart talks about the lack of new images of future clothing, the love of vintage and the old trend of gender-neutral. Jacqueline Sealy, lecturer in bespoke tailoring at London College of Fashion argues that the labour of love, inherent to tailoring, cannot be replaced by robots. Adventurer and environmentalist David de Rothschild speaks about his season-free brand "the lost explorer" and how technology could make the clothing industry more sustainable – and us more self-aware. Linh Le, founder and CEO of the smart textile start-up Bonbouton, explains his belief in functional clothes, which, to him, will be "just clothes" in the future. Richard Sennett, sociologist and author of *The Craftsman* is convinced that handcrafted clothes will gain in importance, as craftsmanship teaches us how to do a good job. Jean Claude Biver, watchmaker and CEO of TAG Heuer S.A., believes that true luxury needs a soul, and explains how companies can achieve it. Gregor Thissen, Executive Chairman of Scabal, believes that clothes will need to work harder in the future to meet the various requirements of our fast lives and wide-ranging interests – which requires a combination of comfort, elegance and longevity. And Yuval Harari finishes with his vision – not particularly on clothes, but on the people or "things" that will wear them, as understanding the future of clothing requires knowing the future of humanity and its advancement.

To shape the world of tomorrow, we have to create spaces of opportunity. For this purpose, we have to imagine where the current changes, if they were to be continued, might lead us. Of course, there is no way to foresee the future and it is likely we will again be surprised, as we were by the COVID-19 pandemic. That is also why at the heart of this experiment is not the practicability of the new technologies and trends, but their desirability. This book concludes with a look into possible futures with seven illustrated scenarios (⟼ Chapter III, p. 137), alongside the exclusive Salvador Dali illustrations on the future of clothing from the 1970s. How realistic are these new visions of the future? How desirable? What are the consequences, risks, chances? This publication is intended to spark a dialogue.

Simone Achermann | W.I.R.E.

THE GENTLEMAN OF THE FUTURE

VISIONS OF THE 21ST CENTURY
BY SALVADOR DALI

To envision the future requires also looking back in time. Many seemingly new developments have their roots in the past – in people's minds. In the early 1970s the surrealist painter Salvador Dali created a series of illustrations on the future of clothing. The twelve pieces of art* reflect his personal vision of fine men's clothing for the 21st century and show clear analogies to the current developments. Many of the suits and accessories, despite their surreal character, reveal a high functionality combined with individualised aesthetics: clothes as living pieces of art enhancing our lives, such as a hat filled with helium to improve the condition of people with depression, shoes with springback heels to walk like an angel on mercury or a dress with attached cassettes, storing the entire history of civilisation on microfilm. The plunge into these past images of the future is ideally combined with a glimpse into today's visions of tomorrow (Chapter IV).

* This book features an exclusive selection of Salvador Dali's work, illustrated in 1971 for Scabal.

"A splendid outfit is not just put on, it must be displayed. It calls for a certain flourish, an aristocratic attitude that represents its quality. A dull outfit has never highlighted a personality."

SALVADOR DALÍ

THE STYLISH FOOTMAN IN THE SERVICE OF A VAGRANT

A PLASTIC AND MICA HAT FILLED WITH HELIUM ELEVATING THE SPIRTS OF DEPRESSED BEGGARS AND MANIACS

"An extravagant outfit can never be effeminate. On the contrary, the urge to be the most handsome and the best dressed indicates a fighting instinct in a man, and shows that he is far more virile than he who merges and succumbs into the grey faceless masses."

SALVADOR DALÍ

I

TOWARDS AUTOMATION, SUSTAINABILITY AND INDIVIDUALITY

DRIVERS OF CHANGE & CASES

Sewing robots, fading dress codes, customers as designers and clothes that think: In the last years, clothing has been undergoing massive change in terms of production and function. New technologies are increasing efficiency in manufacturing and allow the part-individualisation of mass products. The miniaturisation of sensors turns ordinary garments into smart devices. And blurring class, age and gender distinctions are revising old clothing traditions, paving the way for a truly individualised future. At the same time, change seems slow. Smart clothes are still a tiny niche, manufacturing highly personnel dependent and standardisation ubiquitous. Time to have look at the recent developments and their potential for the future.

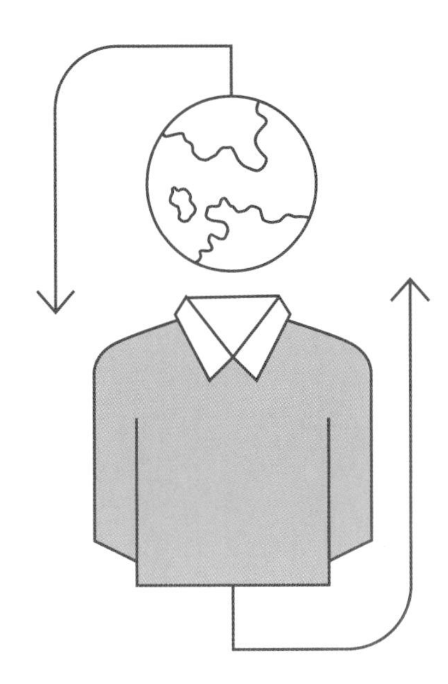

SUSTAINABILITY

More ecological awareness and the increasing knowledge of the massive impact of the clothing industry have led to a growing demand and market for sustainable clothing in the last decade. Whereas for several years it has been a niche for a tiny ecologically aware clientele, mostly produced by small local manufacturers, sustainability is becoming a vital driver of change in the field of clothing. On the one hand, consumer behaviour is changing rapidly. The young in particular are interested in sustainable solutions; 66 percent of global Millennials are willing to spend more on brands that are sustainable.[4] Also, more and more people are profiting from new platforms offering clothing rental, sharing or exchange options. On the other hand, increased transparency over modes of production and labour conditions, as well as the opportunity to use sustainability as a source of differentiation, have caused fashion companies to embrace the importance of sustainability. Some are offering sustainable product brands amongst their conventional supply, others take a pioneering role to convince customers, such as Patagonia, who have built up a loyal clientele through a steady focus on sustainable solutions. A few high street labels are currently experimenting with new brand concepts around longevity, with an emphasis on enduring design and quality. Another important topic will be the issue of waste. Various suppliers of cheap fashion have installed collection bins across their stores, others are starting programs to mend or resew clothes for reuse.

In the next years, the development towards transparency and sustainability will be accelerated by advancements in technology across materials and processes. Examples range from microbes supposed to break down polyester for re-use in new textiles to bacteria produced dyes, which are both currently being tested in the lab for their utility. In addition, virtualisation of the design process and the fitting will render the process of creating physical samples obsolete, which will massively reduce the waste of fabric. Moreover, the increase of blockchain solutions will be a possibility to ensure better transparency. By creating a "digital twin"[5] of each product the journey of a garment will be tracked and, theoretically, any change in custody recorded on the blockchain. Despite the many potential opportunities for companies across the entire value chain and the steps that have already been taken towards more sustainability, it will still be possible to earn money without being sustainable and price will remain a convincing argument in the future. Also, the demand for ecological products has laid the foundations for non-ecological suppliers to "greenwash" their products, which will not always be easy to separate from the truly sustainable goods.

LONG-TERM EFFECTS

— *Sustainability as new standard; requirement of specific differentiation for brands to position themselves as trendsetters in sustainability.*

— *Increasing contribution of clothing to reduce humanity's ecological footprint by substituting resource intensive and environmentally harmful materials and by intensifying transparency on the value chain.*

— *Higher costs and complexity for suppliers to produce sustainably and increase transparency, higher price of clothes for customers.*

— *Risk of greenwashing in context of a growing demand for ecological products, loss of transparency for the buyer.*

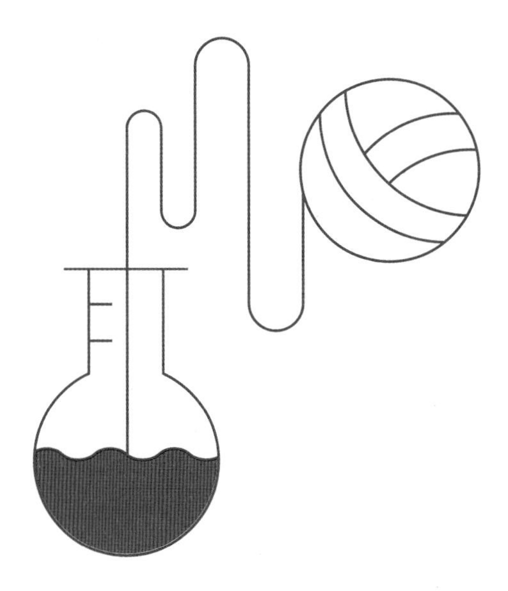

NEW MATERIALS

In the context of the strive for more sustainability and the functionalization of textiles, much of the innovation in the field of clothing has centred on materials. One cornerstone is the substitution or improvement of materials with a big ecological foot print such as cotton, being very water and pesticide intensive, or nylon, which releases poisonous gases in production. On the one hand, much effort has been put into the invention of new, manmade fabrics. Examples range from artificial spider silk, made of a hydrogel consisting of water, silica and cellulose, which proves to be extra strong and flexible, to leather grown in the lab – both currently being tested for their utility. On the other hand, the search for alternative natural materials is becoming increasingly important. The fast-growing, robust hemp is seen as a strong candidate, as it requires very little water and hardly any pesticides. Also lotus fibres, which are not only light weight and soft, but also stain-resistant, are finding their way into textile manufacturing. In addition, new ways of using waste are being developed, such as coffee fibres made of coffee ground or plastic bottles turned into work clothes and uniforms. Another new post-consumer material in development is Karta-Pack™, made of recycled cotton from discarded jeans and shirts, which is said to feel like cotton but with the rigidity of plastic. The other cornerstone of the development of new material is smart fabric – the augmentation of ordinary fabric with integrated functionality. In a first phase, sensors have been attached, later integrated into the textile, without changing the base material. In the recent years, however, ways have been developed to miniaturize sensors so they can be woven directly into the fibre. One material that can be used for this purpose is graphene, a thin and flexible nanomaterial, which can be formed into molecularly small sensors. Besides integrated technology, the imitation or use of nature is playing an important role in the development of smart materials. Textile technologists are also experimenting with fabric made of squid teeth, that can heal itself when put into water. Also, there are various attempts to produce virus- and bacteria-resistant material, for example by imitating the diamond-like texture of shark skin.

As the various projects working on the development of new materials reveal, the future of clothing will be characterised by a shift in terms of the fabric used for clothes. Yet despite the progress that will be made in the coming years, the pace might be slowed down by the many safety tests new fabrics will have to undergo. Long-term side effects for the environment and human health will have to be evaluated, which could be an inhibiting factor for the quick implementation of many products. The disposal of material with integrated technology will pose a challenge, as the different components will first have to be disassembled. Also, some of the man-made or alternative natural fabrics, despite their benefits for the environment, might cause allergies for some wearers. Moreover, much will be invested in the improvement of the fabrication of existing materials; currently many projects are focused on making cotton farming more sustainable.

LONG-TERM EFFECTS

— Further functionalisation of clothing due to the facilitated fusing of electronics with fabrics as a result of miniaturised sensors.

— Acceleration of making clothing sustainable thanks to the application of ecologically harmless materials and a decreasing use of natural resources.

— Potential for the fashion industry to increase creativity with new materials, such as shape-shifting nanomaterials or colour changing electronic materials.

— Chances for other geographical regions and agricultures to profit from the industry due to the use of alternative materials, such as coffee, hemp or lotus fibres; loss of market share and jobs in regions producing conventional fabrics, such as cotton.

— Necessity to test the new materials with regard to long-term consequences for health and the environment and possible risk of premature market entry.

BLURRING GENDER ROLES

Until recently the Western world has been marked by a strong gender binary in clothing: Pants for men, skirts for women. The pursuit of gender equality and a steadily growing number of working women has narrowed the role of clothes in reflecting gender difference. What began with the popularity of jeans in the 1960s in the contect of the youth revolution and the women's liberation movement, has now reached a point at which men and women are hardly separated by their clothes. Whereas the feminisation of male garments has been confined to small communities or to accessories, there has been an increasing masculinisation of female garments: jeans and shirt for all. This development is now reaching the next level with gender-neutral clothing. Whereas streetwear is still emphasising female or male body features, gender neutral garments differentiate through new cuts, frequently oversize, and styles, which fit men and women alike. Several high-end designers have championed gender-neutral clothing and a couple of smaller companies run by young designers are pushing the idea that men's and women's clothes should be obsolete categories, such as the US label Wildfang.[6]

Whereas today gender-neutral is still a niche, it will shape the future of clothing in the next years. First signs are the fact that the approach is starting to hit the high street; H&M and Zara are currently experimenting with small non-gendered ranges. Moreover, gender-neutral garments for children are leading the way into a genderless future of clothing. Big department stores like John Lewis are replacing their former gendered collections with gender-neutral children's clothes.[7] Despite these developments, it should be kept in mind that the tradition to express gender through clothing – even if it has been done in different ways in different cultures – is as old as clothing itself. So it is likely that the future will be marked by a coexistence of gender neutral and gendered clothing. Also, as a reaction to the blurring gender binary in clothing, there may be a new trend towards a more explicit representation of gender. The vintage trend, especially 50s and 60s clothing, which is based on a clear gender binary, is a sign of this development. From the new gentlemen and the girly girls to the committed wearers of gender-neutral clothing – all will be accepted.

LONG-TERM EFFECTS

— Contribution to the current redefinition of femininity and masculinity in clothing and beyond, resulting in a growing importance of clothing as social driver, e.g. in increasing equal chances in working and private environments.

— Search for new styles and shapes focused on personality instead of gender, resulting in new markets and bigger variety; this is a challenge and chance for designers to think about clothing beyond gender.

— Development of a third gender-neutral department next to the gendered sections, mainly consisting of expensive design clothes, adding to additional sales; at the same time there's a new potential to share clothes with friends, lovers or siblings regardless of gender, reducing the investments in clothing.

— Increased comfort and self-esteem for people with no wish or confidence to stage their gender attributes.

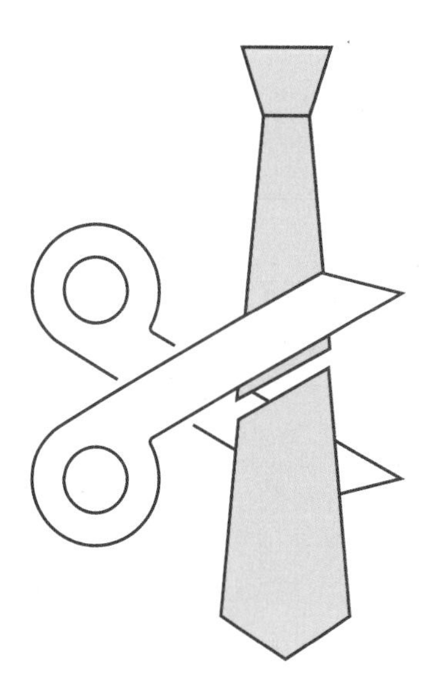

INDIVIDUALISATION AND FADING FORMALITY

In the last decades we have witnessed an ongoing dressing down in private and working environments. Blurring class distinctions, flattening hierarchies, a growing number of people working from their home offices – much more so in post-pandemic times – as well as the orientation of the market on the increasingly young customers have led to a steady casualisation of clothing and the loosening of dress codes. What has started with the introduction of the Casual Friday in business environments or the abolition of compulsory black for funerals has been followed by the triumph of streetwear.

Whereas men used to invest a vital part of their clothing budget for suits, today the most bought men's wear are t-shirts and jeans – even though men spend more on their clothes than ten years ago.[8]

This trend is likely to continue and intensify in the next years. New trends such as athleisure – fashionable sport clothing worn to the office and bar alike – or the pyjama trend, allowing people to walk in public wearing their pyjamas, are signs of a future with even more comfort for the wearer and more liberty to choose how to dress. The decision what to wear and for which occasion will be in the hands of the wearer. As a result, garments will become powerful means to represent our various identities and beliefs in the future. This means that traditional dress codes will not simply be abolished but replaced by new ones. As the fragmentation of society reflects, belonging remains important, it is just shifting from class and geography to various interest groups.

Clothes will represent participation in these new communities through distinct styles and the corresponding new dress codes: from the environmentalist, over the vintage fan to the stay-at-home father. And even if birth, profession and wealth will be less represented by some, others will celebrate them more explicitly – out of conviction not necessity. Suit, tie and gown will survive as strong statements against the casualisation of clothing.

LONG-TERM EFFECTS

— More comfort for the wearer due to the decreasing use of stiff suits, ties and high-heels, especially advantageous for elderly people or people with restricted mobility.

— More freedom of choice for the individual, leading either to an increasing casualisation and the ubiquity of sportswear or to an overall less standardised appearance of clothing, reflecting the increasingly heterogeneous society.

— Less transparency in terms of hierarchies and social status due to the absence of compulsory dress codes; emergence of new markets due to the search for new status symbols outside clothing.

— Loss of market share for suppliers of traditional formal clothing in favour of comfortable clothing, such as streetwear and sports suits, but also a chance to reinterpret and redesign formal clothing and develop new markets.

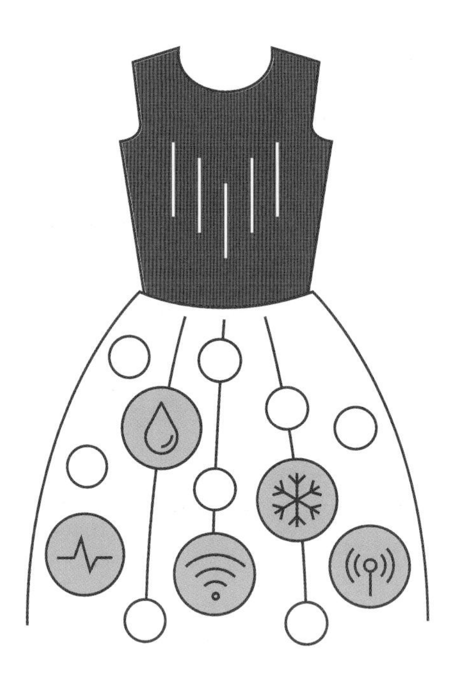

FUNCTIONALISATION

The first serious attempts to merge electronic components and clothing date back to the 1990s, when the first prototypes of e-textiles appeared for military use, developed by MIT students. Today, in the context of an aging society and the emergence of a digital infrastructure, consisting of connected houses, cars – and soon robots, so-called "smart clothing" has left the prototype phase. Whereas until recently the cell phone was seen as the best tool to control our intelligent environment and check our health, functional clothes are now seen as the number one candidate for these tasks. Products already available range from smart yoga pants,[9] helping the wearer to do the positions correctly, to a bikini that warns the wearer if they're at risk of too much sun exposure[10] and the famous smart jacket Jacquard[11] by Google and Levis', which can control the iPhone and play music when the wearer rides a bike or drives a car. The health and beauty industry is currently investing heavily in functional clothing, ranging from prototypes of garments regularly checking the wearer's health or releasing drugs for people with chronic diseases, over integrated pedometers to fight obesity, to clothes with moisturiser or anti-aging ingredients. Performance enhancing clothes are also about to find their way into extreme sports, such as garments helping to regulate body temperature,[12] for example, with the help of warm and cold air, circulating through a network of tiny tubes embedded in the undershirt. At the far end of the spectrum are the experiments with protective clothing that guard the wearer against radiation or the risks of space travel, such as deadly solar particles.[13] Fashion is also taking advantage of functional textiles with dresses that shiver and mutate under the gaze of others or textiles that can change colour through gathering energy from body vibrations or heat, all of which, however, is still mostly confined to fashion shows or art exhibitions.

Whereas much of the connected clothing has been confined to small niche markets or is still facing various test phases, some of the products could hit the mass market in the near future. Progress in electronics, making the smartness in smart clothing invisible through the miniaturisation of sensors, as well as reduced costs of production as a result of increased experience will be beneficial for this development. However, the fear of further dependence on technology and the risk of invasions privacy through external control could nevertheless stir consumer scepticism and prevent a proper breakthrough. Nevertheless, for elderly people, or people with chronic diseases clothes with health controlling or drug releasing functions could be useful and the corresponding products and markets successful.

LONG-TERM EFFECTS

— *Growing dispersion of functional clothes for specific market segments such as sports and health purposes, based on the increasing number of chronic patients; ultimately broadening towards clothes taking over the role of smart phones, for example for communication and identification for payments.*

— *Risk of data loss due to data hacking of wearable sensors in clothes and the need to include cyber security strategies into clothing.*

— *Increasing collaboration and emergence of knowledge and products at the interface of clothing, communication technology, safety, healthcare and beauty, such as drug releasing suits or dresses that can account for the identity of the owner.*

— *Potential for early detection of potential illnesses or nutrient deficiencies, chance of better and longer health for the wearer and society as a whole; need for services that help with analysing the health data.*

— *Further dependency on technology for the individual and risk of violation of the wearer's privacy due to potential hacking of personal data and the pressure exercised by insurance providers to make their customers wear health controlling clothes.*

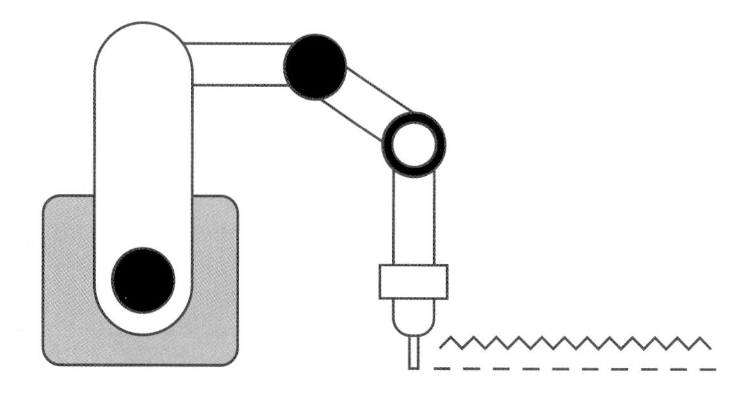

AUTOMATION

Historically, the clothing sector has been at the forefront of automation. The Power Loom, the first mechanised loom, was a key development in the industrial revolution. Nevertheless, garment production has been slow in adapting to the latest technology. Availability of cheap labour and the high initial investment for machines have kept the fabrication of garments extremely personnel dependent. In recent years, however, with the growth in global demand for clothing, the trend towards fast fashion and a stiff international competition, the industry's attitude shifted. The range of jobs carried out by machines now extends from small tasks such as bobbin change, over automated ironing to knife cutting systems and cutting room management software, able to command and track production activities and provide reports for future planning. The realisation of the last but most important step towards fully automated fabrication of garments still poses a major challenge, though. The main reason is that material handling is complicated: it is flexible, it warps, it folds – something only human hands have been able to deal with. However, a new generation of intelligent sewing robots, which mimic the jobs done by people, is paving the way to tackle this last task. "Sewbot" by the US company Softwear Automation, for example, uses a highly calibrated machine vision system that analyses fabric more accurately than the human eye and determines the exact needle placement. Robotic arms then continually manipulate and adjust the fabric to be properly arranged. A different approach to accelerate automation is the use of glue instead of seams, which not only facilitates the production of waterproof garments due to the absence of puncture holes but also makes the use of sewing robots obsolete. Besides the production of garments, design of clothing, trend prediction, and purchase are being automated, alongside customer advice with the help of artificial intelligence (AI). Algorithms and keyword search are crawling through videos, social media and blogs to detect the latest trends and lay the base for the purchase department and for the creation of new garments. For the customer, intelligent recommendation platforms, analysing their personal style, are taking over the role of the sales person in the store. However, the performance of machine learning is limited, as it is confined to repetitive processes: recommendations are based on past behaviour, AI Design on recombining already existing patterns.

In the coming years, it is likely that the fabrication of many garments will be fully automated due to improved sewing technologies. The consequences will be increased efficiency, cheaper production and lower prices for the customer. Due to the reduction of human resources, some of the production will be shifted back to high wage countries. The shortened supply chains from the supplier to the client will lead to more sustainability. The cheaper manufacturing, however, could result in more production and more fast fashion. Also, complete automation brings its risks: malfunctioning machines could lead to great losses and companies are open to attack through hacking. Moreover, whereas automation could prove to be beneficial for wealthy countries, for low wage areas it could mean a great loss of jobs. In terms of the use of artificial intelligence, the gains will be more efficiency in reproducing existing designs and consumer behavior, new insights and styles, however, are less likely.

LONG-TERM EFFECTS

— Cheaper and faster production of garments due to the higher speed of machines and the reduction of human resources, higher affordability of clothes for the customer.

— Shifting of the clothing industry to high wage countries, smaller ecological footprint due to the proximity of production and consumption, major loss of jobs in low wage countries.

— Risk of poor quality and great losses due to malfunctioning machines and hacking attacks.

— Loss of variety in styles due to the use of intelligent algorithms for design, purchase and recommendation tools, based on the repetition of already existing patterns.

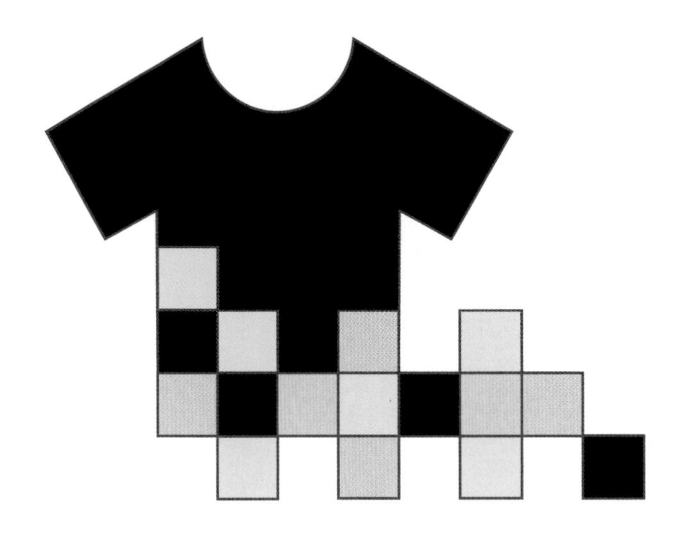

VIRTUALISATION

In recent years, virtualisation has had a large impact on the efficiency of the clothing industry. Traditionally, the clothing production chain starts with an idea put on paper and ends with physical pieces presented to customers. This chain consists of many steps that are no longer necessarily made by hand. Computer-aided design (CAD) is used right from the design initiation and production stage through lay planning, spreading, patternmaking, cutting, and finally sewing. Pattern design software has facilitated patternmaking and grading and created digital pattern libraries for future retrieval. Further progress in the field is being made with three-dimensional (3D) software, permitting 3D visualization of drape and fit on virtual models or avatars, thereby rendering the process of physical sample generation unnecessary. Moreover, 3D scanning and mapping customised avatars in accordance with specific body and facial features is now paving the way for customised mass garments. A second area which virtualisation is about to reform is online fitting and shopping. The number of online purchases has radically increased and is likely to further climb in the future, especially in the late post-pandemic context. Improvements in technology, such as 3D body scanning, will also play a major role in this development. Over recent decades bulky and costly 3D body scanners have evolved into affordable, accurate and handy devices. The 3D scans form a digital copy of the outside of the body and can be interfaced with the clothing patterns, a process called "virtual fitting". Until recently, the fitting has been confined to static body postures. Now virtual fitting rooms are being created using a depth sensor, which provides a realistic fitting experience with customised motion filters, size adjustments and physical simulation. Another big field in which virtualisation will play a leading role is virtual clothing for avatars. What started with the fashionable avatar-dresses in the famous game *Second Life* is not only expanding to other games but also to the many avatars that will be used in digital communication, healthcare and education. The beginning of this phase in the evolution of digital clothing was seen in the first Metaverse Fashion Week, which took place in early 2022.

As the many advantages of virtualisation suggest, it will play a major role in shaping the future of clothing. In the next years, CAD programs will be perfected, which will lead to better efficiency and less waste. Yet despite the various chances, there will be some challenges to be tackled. The possibility to try out endless variations of design could also lead to inefficiency. The most important limitation, however, will be the detachment from the material reality for the customer, e.g. the loss of the use of the senses when trying and buying clothes online. So far, there is no technology available than can imitate this physical experience. Therefore, it is unlikely that virtualisation will make stores or other places in which garments can be felt completely obsolete – which may be reflected in online supplier Zalando's decision to open its own physical stores. In this context, the role of retail stores will be redefined: At the centre the physical experience and the exchange with the personnel – supported by digital technologies that enhance the customer's journey. And whereas virtualisation will not entirely replace old markets, it will create new ones: Once we all develop our own avatars for business and private communication, as demonstrated by the CEO of the Swiss bank UBS,[14] we will need clothing which fits our personality.

LONG-TERM EFFECTS

— Better efficiency and cheaper production of clothes as no physical samples have to be created, reduction of waste and the overall ecological footprint of the industry.

— Better quality and growth of online shopping due to 3D fitting programs, decrease of the number of physical shops.

— Loss of material experience for customers; redefinition of the store and its functions, the focus shifting from the display of a multitude of styles and colours to the sensual experience of the garment.

— Potential for designers to try out various styles with a relatively low investment of time and effort. This could lead to a greater variety of designs, but with the risk of too much choice leading to a setback in efficiency.

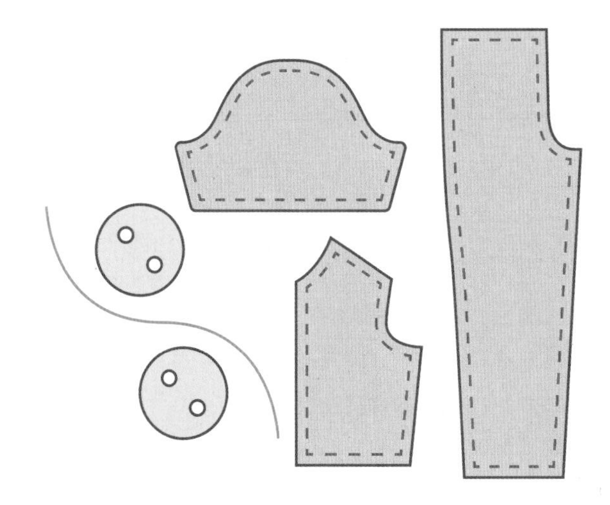

DEMOCRATISATION OF PRODUCTION

With the emergence of mass consumer products, people have become passive buyers of readymade clothing. Homemade clothes have not only become unnecessary, they also lost their attraction in comparison to the new and shiny products from the store. In the last decade, this development has been successively reverted with the growing do-it-yourself trend in clothing and beyond. Among the reasons are a growing distrust towards the industry and its opaque production chains, the rejection of mass-produced products in times of individualisation and the desire to create tangibles in the digital age. What started with a few ecologically aware and manually skilled young people turned into a thriving DIY community, exchanging tips from maker to maker and proudly presenting their self-made clothes online. Meanwhile, not only to make but also to buy self-made is regarded highly among young customers, as the success of platforms selling self-made clothes and accessories like Etsy or DaWanda shows. Moreover, readymade clothes, if still bought, are increasingly being individualised by the wearer. Online clothing-hack videos are teaching people how to re-style mass-produced products with buttons and zippers and how to re-use or upcycle worn out garments.

In the next couple of years, new technologies such as 3D printers and computer aided design systems (CAD) might further promote the DIY trend. The first prototypes of home 3D printers for textiles[15] and the attempts to make design software easier to use could enable people with little time or manual skills to create their own dress in the future. In this context, and as a result of the continuing move towards individualisation, the traditional hierarchy between the customer and the supplier is starting to fade. Customers want their personalities to be mirrored in their garments – either by taking part in the design process or by actively shaping the brand's identity. Big suppliers are reacting with affordable mass-made-to-measure garments, which take into account people's measurements and unique touches, like stitched-in initials into the production process. Some start-ups like Original Stitch[16] are experimenting with the idea to turn the customer into a designer with the help of personalised recommendations, 3D measuring and fitting. Others are embracing this shift in power by placing their reputation fully into the hands of the people, where it is moulded in the blogs of customers and online influencers. With this increasing democratisation of clothing, the appetite for small labels will grow to the detriment of megabrands such as PPR's Gucci and LVMH's Louis Vuitton, which have already seen their sales growth slow, even in vibrant markets such as China.[17] The result of these changes will be less standardised clothing that reflects people's identities and the mood of the society. Among the downsides will be the time-effort of DIY design, the safety tests for the new materials used for 3D printing and the heterogeneous quality of self- or semi-self made goods, in many cases lagging behind the century's long expertise of the industry.

LONG-TERM EFFECTS

— Shrinking market for standardised mass-produced products, chances for small suppliers and unknown designers to participate in the industry, need for big suppliers to adapt their goods to customer's wishes.

— Chance for increased creativity and emergence of truly new styles due to the greater number and different types of designers.

— Higher identification of customers with their self-made or semi self-made clothes and their customer-influenced brands.

— Heterogeneous quality of self-made clothes due to lack of experience, time-consuming involvement of the individual in the design and fabrication process.

THE REAL ONESIE

One simple way to reduce the industry's ecological footprint is to reduce the amount of clothing produced and consumed. Annually, over 100 billion pieces of clothing find their way into the stores, approximately 15 new outfits per person per year. Yet despite an increasing ecological awareness, most people are not willing to abstain from changing their looks. To reconcile the requirements of sustainability and the customers' needs, some companies have started to create clothes that can be worn for any occasion. This no longer only involves making garments with classic, timeless silhouettes, but also creating pieces that can morph with a few tweaks to create outfits that look different. The brands Aday, Misha Nonoo® and Amour Vert are experimenting with transformable garments in different price categories, from an oversize blazer, that can be worn as part of a suit, as a light overcoat or as mini-dress – to a wrap dress that can be wrapped in various ways, each changing the degree of elegance and body accentuation. To guarantee its frequent use and comfort, the designers' focus lies on material and colour. Most pieces are in neutral black, white and grey to fit any occasion and any other garment, and are made of high-tech synthetic fabrics that need no ironing and allow a swift change of look. Though the idea of a versatile wardrobe seems to make total sense, a proper breakthrough in the future could be frustrated by the simple fact that less clothing makes less money.

→ thisisaday.com
→ mishanonoo.com
→ amourvert.com

NEVER GETTING DIRTY...

A quarter of a garment's carbon footprint over the course of its lifetime comes from cleaning it; washing machines account for almost a fifth of our home water usage.[18] There are two ways to reduce these numbers: creating products that stay clean longer and changing people's hygiene practices – it is estimated that 90% of clothes washed are not dirty enough to be thrown in the laundry.[19] The first approach appears faster, which is why several new suppliers focus on the innovation of clothes that need only rare washing or no washing at all. In both cases, the material is crucial: it should be more resistant to odour and dirt. To achieve this, the start-up Unbound Merino relies on wool, which is naturally breathable and moisture-absorbing, preventing the sweat from remaining in the shirt. To bypass the wool-feel, ultra fine Merino is used to fabricate soft and thin garments, ideal for summer shirts, underwear and socks. The eco-friendly brand Pangaia created a mix of organic cotton and renewable seaweed fibre, which it treats with peppermint oil for its antibacterial properties and a fresh feel. A more technological approach is adopted by the start-ups Threadsmiths and LABFRESH, which take the wash-less philosophy further with their stain-resistant shirts. While Threadsmiths works with a hydrophobic coating based on nanotechnology, LABFRESH uses a secret formula to repel liquids from red wine to hot chocolate sauce and to resist bacteria from sweat. The downside: nano-textiles have yet to be tested for long-term effects on health. Another obstacle to wash-less and no-wash garments: people will want to clean them no matter what. A first step to reverse this culture could be new washing tags that advise people to relax.[20]

→ https://unboundmerino.com
→ https://thepangaia.com/collections/shop-all/products/t-shirt
→ https://www.thethreadsmiths.com
→ https://labfresh.eu/pages/technology

White business shirt, unharmed by the red wine spilled on it, LABFRESH.

Picture: © Marc Haers provided by LABFRESH

THE WEARER OF TOMORROW

Clothing is changing, as are its wearers. Fashion's embracement of artificial intelligence and technology reached a first peak with a new generation of digitally rendered avatars. At the forefront of this development was the computer-generated influencer Miquela Sousa, created back in 2016, now commanding a following of 3 million. The perpetually 19-year-old quickly made the leap from a novelty internet sensation to a legitimate industry player: in 2018 brands like Prada, Chanel and Supreme dressed her, her face was seen on the front page of fashion magazines like *Vogue*. Another notable digital personality is Noonoouri, a manga-like luxury lifestyle player, dressed in the looks of Dior, Jacquemus, and Off-White™. While Miquela and Noonoouri fit the category of influencer-model, other avatars act more like traditional mannequins, such as the realistic-looking Black model Shudu, promoted by The Diigitals, the first digital modelling agency. Shudu's potential was on show at the 2019 BAFTA-Awards in London, where the holographic digital supermodel acted as an AI stylist, capturing the styles of the stars and serving up the looks for people at home to shop. Swarovski®, BAFTA's official jewellery partner, designed her bespoke digital gown, made up of tens of thousands of double pointed chaton crystals in different shades of yellow.

Digital fashion influencer Noonoouri with a doll-like appearance but a real impact on the fashion world.

Will fashion avatars have a larger impact on clothing and society as a whole? Their creators claim they will champion diversity in the fashion world and collaborate with designers from emerging economies and under-represented communities. However, the perfect bodies, the flawless faces and the creation of Black female characters by white male designers has understandably given rise to controversy.[21] Either way: fashion avatars and digital fashion shows are on the rise and designers will enter a whole new terrain to dress them.

The first digital supermodel Shudu, who appeared on the red carpet at the British Academy Film Awards in 2019. Courtesy of @shudu.gram and @thediigitals.

→ https://www.thediigitals.com/shudu
→ https://www.instagram.com/shudu.gram/?hl=en
→ https://www.standard.co.uk/tech/baftas-shopping-ai-5g-ee-a4061436.html
→ https://www.joergzuber.com
→ https://www.instagram.com/noonoouri/?hl=de

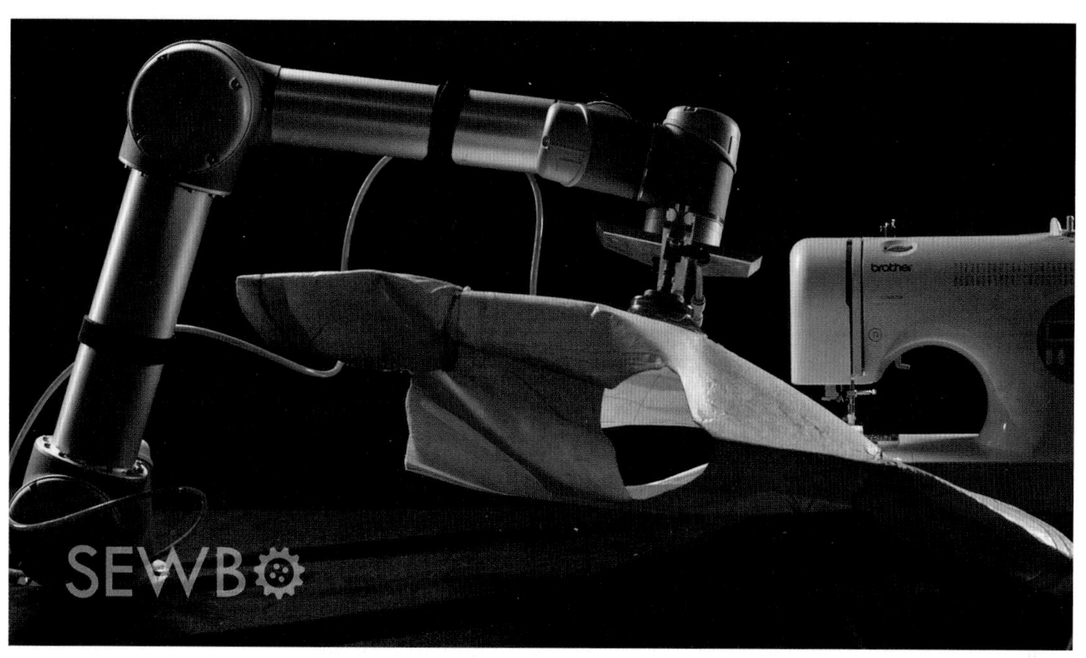

"SEWBO", the first sewing robot to have sewn together an entire t-shirt, Sewbo.

ROBOTS THAT SEW

Over the last few decades, many tasks of garment manufacturing have been automated, yet putting together the final piece of clothing has not been one of them. This is because working with limp and flexible textiles requires special skills; basically hands that continuously put the cloth in the right position – something robots have failed at until recently. The start-up Sewbo was the first to produce a fully robotically sewn garment by temporarily stiffening the fabric with a thermoplastic coating. This should also allow off-the-shelf robots to "build" garments from rigid cloth, just as if they were working with sheet metal. At the end of the manufacturing process, the water-soluble stiffener is removed with a simple rinse in hot water. Another approach is taken by the machine vision and robotics start-up called Softwear Automation, which is trying to imitate and accelerate the kind of work humans are doing: Their sewing robot LOWRY uses high-speed cameras to map the fabric and various robotic arms to steer it through the sewing needles. Though initially only able to make simple products, such as bath mats, the technology has become advanced enough to make whole t-shirts. Various apparel companies, such as Adidas, are meanwhile relying on their robots. The reasons are obvious: From cutting to sewing a shirt, it takes only four minutes; and working under the guidance of a single human handler, the robot can make as many shirts per hour as around 17 employees. Even though it seems clear that this new generation of sewing robots will pave the way into a fully automated future, they are still far from making fine garments such as suits or evening gowns. These will remain in the hands of humans - for now.

→ www.sewbo.com
→ softwearautomation.com/products/
→ http://trendintech.com/2016/11/01/amazing-sewing-robot-makes-clothes-right-in-front-of-you/

I FASHION

A fast-growing global DIY sewing community and the continuous virtualisation of fashion design have led to an explosion in design software programs for home use. Originally built for professionals, various companies have opened up their platforms for hobby designers. The promise is to simplify the design process and to allow users to quickly build their skills and develop wearable garments. The fashion design software Tailornova, for example, assists people with drawing technical sketches, turns their measurements into a 3D virtual model, offers pre-views of their sketch on that model and eventually transforms the chosen design into made-to-measure sewing patterns – ready to download, cut and sew. This allows people to create several designs within minutes, without having to redraw and cut. That said: Designing a dress or trousers from scratch and sewing them together requires a skilled hand and years of practice. To meet the needs of beginners, other platforms such as Apliiq offer pre-designed clothes, which are customised online with hoods, pockets, colours or personal artworks printed on the textiles. Once they're done designing, the customer purchases the items – which are then made and delivered by Apliiq. For those who prefer to witness the actual making of their clothing there is the walk-in design studio and store as established by Ministry of Supply, which specialises in functional business clothing. Customers enter their store, choose from various shapes, colours and buttons and witness their garment "printed" in front of them with a 3D robotic knitting machine. Although most people will still buy most of their clothing from the shelf in the future, the new tools for DIY clothing will certainly lead to a bigger variety in styles and less standardisation.

→ tailornova.com
→ www.apliiq.com
→ www.ministryofsupply.com

DRUG-RELEASING CLOTHES

One of the major challenges in treating chronic disease is the fact that patients often forget to take their drugs. Another challenge is the need for a change in dosage is usually only recognised during regular check ups at the doctor's, rather than instantaneously when the body needs it. A promising approach to overcome these problems comes from an unexpected direction: clothing. In recent years, we have witnessed major advances in material research and a close cooperation of the field with biochemistry.[22] The Swiss Federal Laboratories for Materials Science and Technology (Empa), for example, are currently working on integrating therapeutic drugs into biodegradable polymer fibre. The smart fibres are supposed to recognise the need for therapy and dose the active ingredients with precision. For that purpose, the polymers are designed to degrade only under certain conditions, for example at the occurrence of hypoglycemia in the case of diabetes. Moreover, drug-releasing materials are also designated for the treatment of injuries, which the fibres are supposed to recognise, for example, by an altered pH value of the skin indicating that tissue damage must be treated or an infected wound cured with antibiotics. The long-term plan of the researchers is to use these fibres in ordinary textiles and garments. This would not only dramatically improve the quality of life of patients, it would also be a huge relief for healthcare. Until today, however, the understanding of the interactions between biomaterials and the body are limited; searching through the vast realm of materials to get minimal toxicity and maximal preservation of the bioactivity of the drug will take years of research.[23] The shirt that will cure your headache is unlikely to hit the high street anytime soon.

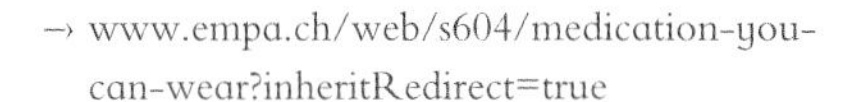
→ www.empa.ch/web/s604/medication-you-can-wear?inheritRedirect=true

Biodegradable, drug-releasing material used for the project "Self Care Materials", Empa.

THE 100 YEAR PANTS

The "100 Year Pants", fireproof and water-resistant male pants supposed to last more than a lifetime, Vollebak.

The life expectancy of a garment heavily depends on its material and how often it is worn. As a majority of people use just a small part of their wardrobe, in Europe and the US on average 30 percent,[24] the wear and tear on our most popular garments can be very high. This is more of a problem with the generally decreasing quality of clothing as a result of cheap and fast production: meaning cotton trousers are worn out after two years, while a synthetic dress lasts less than one year.[25] Meaning: People are forced to replace their clothes even if they don't want to. There is the option to repair them and help is offered by clothing repair places and services, such as the clothes doctors.[26] Another approach is to make and buy clothes that last – mending bad quality garments being a rather fruitless effort. The start up Vollebak, for example, is producing some men's pants that promise to outlive its owner. To last more than 100 years, they're made with several layers of fabric: the outer being a tear-resistant, water repellent and breathable soft shell, the bottom layer made of a knitted fireproof fibre that should feel like cotton. Another product by the firm is a shirt made of carbon, usually used for missiles and jet engines. Woven with 120 metres of carbon fibre, the shirt is stronger than steel, while being soft and lightweight. Although this is performance clothing, the pants and shirt are designed to be comfortable and simple looking enough for use beyond sports and adventure. The high price is a barrier for many, yet to repeatedly buy new favourites is also expensive – and holds the risk of mistakes, further filling the unused sections of the wardrobe. So the main downside? How to sustainably get rid of indestructible garments. Bequeath them.

→ www.vollebak.com/product/100-year-pants-granite/
→ www.schoeller-textiles.com/de/technologien/pyroshell

VIRTUAL REALITY SHOPPING CENTRE

In 2018, the online apparel industry was responsible for roughly $480 billion in revenues and these numbers are expected to rise to $712.9 billion by 2022.[27] Even though a majority of users state that they merely buy clothes online due to the bigger selection and a higher chance of finding what they are looking for investors believe that a better, more sensual virtual shopping experience will be key to success for labels in the future. The Jeff Bezos backed start-up "Obsess" is determined to make e-shopping more appealing for the eye and claims to be more exciting than a visit to a real store. Their augmented reality and virtual shopping centre consists of 19 stores, each designed along different themes according to the latest trends in fashion: from an underwater store with glass walls and ceiling looking out into the ocean, displaying a selection of coral dresses, to a yoga studio, presenting the latest sports fashion on virtual people doing their exercises. The curated products amount to around 700 items, which customers can explore in virtual reality using their smartphones. The concept aims to move online shopping forward – from a simple search for garments to a joyful process of exploration and discovery. This might win over even more customers to the digital side and put a further threat to the already struggling retailers on the street. However, for now, touch and feel remains in the hands of the analogue world and virtual fitting has yet to prove its effectiveness.

→ https://obsessar.com

The underwater 'Coral Room' of the high-end virtual mall "Obsess".

DRIVERS OF CHANGE

Overview of changing social and environmental context

- 1 -
CONTINUOUS INDIVIDUALISATION

Opening value systems, flexible gender roles, a continuously changing professional world and the ongoing desire for individualisation form the basis for a greater diversity of life models. As a result, the demand for customised clothes and accessories is also increasing, the characteristics of which are intended to do justice to individual lifestyles and values. Data-based applications promise a technological basis for mass customisation, but they can lead to social fragmentation and reach the limits of technological and economic feasibility. At the same time, there is growing pressure on individuals to make the right decisions a huge array of options, resulting in a growing desire for simplicity. To reduce complexity, people will increasingly look towards solutions that offer quick and convenient advice for everything from getting inspiration to shopping. Next to algorithmic recommendations, communities that provide a clear value-based framework will gain in importance.

- 2 -
SEARCH FOR TRANSPARENCY

The internet has allowed people to access and share information more extensively and faster than ever before. This digitally driven transparency makes it harder for companies to act invisibly to the public eye. Unethical or even illegal behaviour becomes riskier with an increased risk of exposure and loss of reputation. In a world where facial recognition technology is applied by government and private companies alike, individual behaviour also becomes more visible and a degree of privacy is lost. Here, clothing can act as protection of people's privacy, by obscuring people's facial characteristics or distorting the algorithms.

- 3 -
INCEASING ROLE OF HEALTH

The ageing of the global population and unhealthy lifestyles make chronic and non-communicable diseases a common occurrence. More people will suffer from chronic diseases that require daily treatment. At the same time, the risk of pandemics such as COVID-19, as well as the danger of the renaissance of old infectious diseases such as malaria due to rising temperatures in Europe, will inform the global society. Therefore, the focus in healthcare shifts towards preventing diseases instead of just treating them. Clothes, as a near constant companion of human beings, are positioned to play a vital role in helping people to protect their bodies and keep track of their health condition.

- 4 -
AUTOMATED PRODUCTION

Algorithmic automation allows for the removal of human influences from processes and task with low complexity and high repetition. Not only does this free up people to do more complex and human-focused tasks, it also makes the goods production and service provision faster and cheaper. However, despite the progress of artificial intelligence, automation of production will mainly change repetitive processes. The potential to outsource complex and new procedures will be limited to low volumes and specialised projects. Still in the large scale of massmarket production digital automation makes it possible for clothing companies to locate their production sites more independently of labour cost and move closer to the demand. Increasingly optimised algorithms will also result in more homogenous output in regard to quality and process. It becomes, therefore, crucial for companies to find alternative ways to differentiate themselves in the market.

- 5 -
SEARCH FOR AUTHENTICITY

As our lives are increasingly dominated by a technology-driven environment, natural solutions are becoming more appealing. Additionally, the subjective feeling of an accelerated world shapes the search for reduction and deceleration. Because of this desire for authenticity and deceleration, local, self- and handmade fashion articles are meeting a growing customer demand.

- 6 -
CRITICAL ENVIRONMENTAL CONDITIONS

Climate change and the worsening environmental pollution sensitises people to the importance of sustainability. As a result, individuals and companies change their behaviour, either voluntarily or are compelled to do so by regulations, social pressure and economic survival. Additionally, extreme weather conditions will become more commonplace. Clothing will take up a crucial role when it comes to the protection from this increasingly hostile environment and a reduction of toxic waste from the traditional ways of production.

- 7 -
QUANTIFICATION

Sensors with higher performance and better diagnostic methods enable more accurate measurement of behaviour, health and environmental factors. Intelligent clothes with integrated sensors and new fabrics will be a part of the data-generating and interconnected environment. The extent to which this will become socially accepted depends on the ability of producers and regulators to ensure secure and ethical data collection.

- 8 -
FOCUS ON SUSTAINABILITY

The increasing consumption of the growing global population puts a strain on natural resources. To avoid resource scarcity or even exhaustion, societal and economic actors are facing the challenge to restructure the production and use of clothes in a more ecologically and socially sustainable fashion.

- 9 -
NEW SIMULATIONS AND VIRTUAL REALITIES

Growing computational power leads to the rise of virtual environments, avatars and real-life simulation as complementary reality for experiences and representation. With the rise of virtual models or influencers or digital twins of citizens or actors, there will be a growing demand to design these digital environments and develop traditional or new types of virtual clothes.

- 10 -
ENHANCED FUNCTIONALISATION

Advancement in robotics and new materials enable human beings to more profoundly enhance their skills and senses, for example with exoskeletons. Clothing becomes more functionalised. Not only does it get increasingly better at serving a specific purpose, it can also take up more and more tasks.

"Everything about man
should be beautiful;
his face and his clothes,
his soul and his thoughts."

SALVADOR DALÍ

MAN OF THE YEAR 2000 WHO WILL BE GASTRONOMICALLY STEREOSCOPIC AND STEREOCHEMICAL

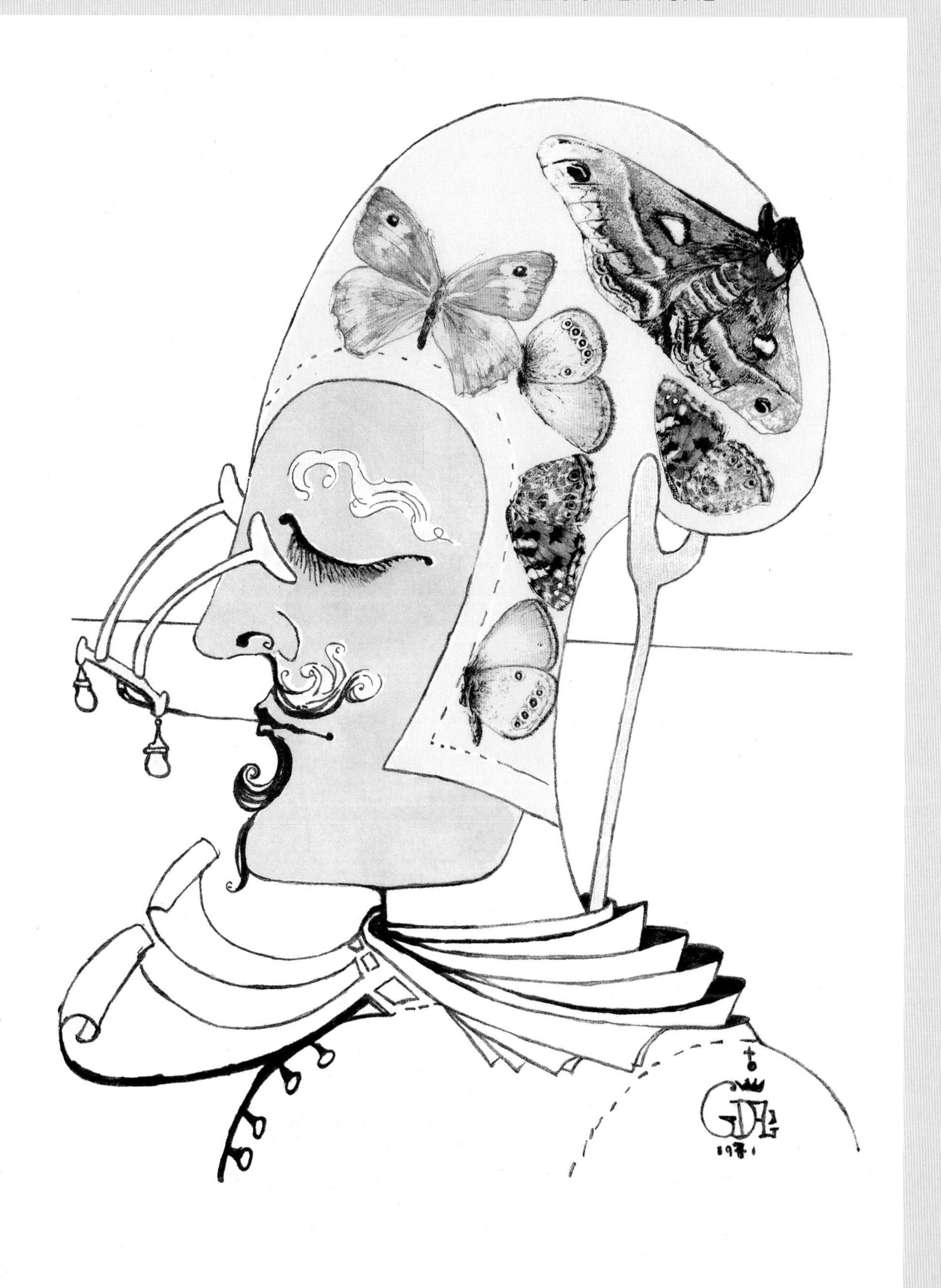

A DANDY WITH PERFECTLY USELESS LYRICAL APPENDAGES

"To be clad is not to be dressed. Clothes screen you from observation and protect you from climate. But dress is part of something far more complex. Dress is influenced by a man's state of mind, his desire to be different, and his longing for luxury. Dress is either an acceptance or rejection of society. The error lies in being clad but not dressed."

SALVADOR DALÍ

II

LOOKING BEYOND FASHION

IDEAS & OPINIONS

Much of the discourse on the future of clothing is centred on new technologies. However, current changes are more far-reaching than this and affect the wider world. What is luxury tomorrow? How does AI design affect individualisation? How can the clothing industry become truly sustainable? What happens to craftsmanship in times of automation? What are the consequences of mass-made-to-measure for bespoke tailoring? What are clothes capable and incapable of doing for us tomorrow? How new are the current changes? And what will the future wearers look like? In this chapter, academics, entrepreneurs and makers discuss the latest developments and share their ideas on the future of clothing.

CULTURE AND GENDER

TIME TO ENVISION THE NEW!

AMBER BUTCHART

The most radical change in the history of clothing has already happened: the fact that most people can afford to buy clothes, says fashion historian Amber Butchart. Many of the current trends, such as gender-neutral garments, have their roots in a distant past. And yet genuine change is in reach – if we don't get stuck in old imagery of the future.

MASS-MADE-TO-MEASURE, FAST FASHION, SMART-CLOTHES, FADING DRESS CODES: ARE WE FACING THE MOST RADICAL CHANGE IN THE HISTORY OF CLOTHING?

No, I do not think so. There have been periods in history when much more change was happening. The industrial revolution, for example, dramatically altered not only the way people worked in the production of clothing but also the affordability of garments. Before the 19th century, the fabrication of clothes was so labour intensive that garments were amongst the most expensive things you could own. People would mention their clothes and textiles in their will and bequeath them to their closest friends or relatives – as they had such enormous value. Improvements in technology since the 18th century, but especially in the 19th century, laid the foundation to make garments increasingly more affordable. From the 1860s seasonal change in clothing was becoming a bigger part of the industry, becoming the fashion calendar that we would recognise today. Now we even have fast fashion replacing seasons. The fabrication of clothes has become so cheap that many people can afford to wear them once and then discard them.

BESIDES TECHNOLOGY: WHAT ARE THE OTHER DRIVERS OF CHANGE THAT SHAPE THE PAST, PRESENT AND FUTURE OF CLOTHING?

Cultural shifts – the way people think; what they consider to be right or wrong, beautiful or ugly. Let's take the famous example of the mini skirt. Before its emergence in the 1960s, at any point in the Western world it would have been unacceptable, even unthinkable, to go out and show that much of your leg. In the context of post-war prosperity, the "sexual revolution" of the contraceptive pill and the baby boom, this shift became possible. Today, we are confronted with climate change. As a result, people are becoming more aware of the ecological effects of their behaviour and of the dramatic impact the clothing industry has on the environment. Such a change in attitude can lead to a cultural shift in consumerism: increasing numbers of people are starting to favour sustainable, high quality clothing over cheap garments. However, cost still remains an issue here for many people. Another example is the shift in how we think about gender, including the legislation of gay marriage – which can impact the way we express masculinity and femininity through clothing.

TALKING OF GENDER AND CLOTHING: HOW SERIOUSLY DO YOU TAKE THE CURRENT TREND TOWARDS GENDER-NEUTRAL?

Ideas of gender and the way people express them through clothing is cultural. If we look at other societies and other times, the expression of gender through garments is not static. The way we gender clothing in the West is historically different from other places in the world. While it is quite unusual for us to see this breakdown in gender binary in terms of the silhouette of clothing, this is not the case elsewhere.

The radical distinction between boys' and girls' clothes is an invention of the 20th century: Prince William (1765–1837), later Duke of Clarence, King William IV, portrayed in a pink dress.

In the West, trousers and skirts have been the way to distinguish between male and female for centuries, whereas in Japan, for example, gender was at times expressed more through fabrication than silhouette. Europe has also seen this absence of distinction between genders, but this was confined to childhood. If we look at 18th century portraits, you may see a young prince, ostensibly dressed as a girl to our eyes, wearing a pink dress. Boys and girls would be dressed in this way until the age of 7 – which was the age a boy was breeched,

> “Clothing will never be a blank flag.”
>
> AMBER BUTCHART

marking the beginning of manhood. Also, the colours blue and pink have not always signified male and female respectively. On the contrary, pink, until the beginning of the 20th century, was seen as a strong, manly colour. The radical distinction between boys’ and girls’ clothes, the way we know it today, is largely the result of the acceleration of marketing. You can sell so much more if you have a boys’ and a girls’ section! Recently, the UK department store John Lewis abolished gendered garments for children. It is not unlikely we might be going back to a gender-free childhood – at least in terms of clothes.

YOU MENTIONED THE DEPICTION OF CLOTHING IN PORTRAITS. WHAT DO WE LEARN ABOUT THE FUTURE OF CLOTHING IN MOVIES?

Costume in science fiction can be intertwined with ideas of extreme fashion to make statements about status and inequality in fictional future worlds. For example, *The Hunger Games* series (2012–present) is a story told in many ways through style: through utilitarian clothing vs outlandish couture – often borrowed from real designers. A similar parallel exists in Gaultier’s designs for *The Fifth Element* (1997). Interestingly, we learn a lot about past visions of the future of clothing too. Even in sci-fi, visions of futuristic clothes are often rooted in the 1960s. The ideas around space age and the Cold War that were formulated then, still largely impact the way we look into the future now. Besides this 60s retro futurism, encapsulated in films such as *Barbarella* (1968) whose costumes were inspired by Paco Rabanne, sci-fi can also draw on the distant past to create the future. For example, *Star Wars* (1977–present), which took inspiration from Samurai warriors' dress. And *Blade Runner* (1982) famously referenced the 1940s and the aesthetics of film noir, and continues to be cited as an inspiration for fashion designers such as Alexander Wang, and previously Alexander McQueen.

PAST IMAGES OF THE FUTURE IN MIND: IS CLOTHING AN AREA THAT IS VISIONARY OR RATHER TRADITIONAL – LIKE FOOD – AS IT IS ANOTHER BASIC NEED?

The depiction of fashion and garments is more visionary than the representation of food in film. The difference is probably based on the fact that food is absolutely a basic need and clothing is less so. Clothes are a powerful way of self-representation and so visions of them need to be more demonstrative. Nevertheless, we sometimes get stuck envisioning the future with images from the past. It is time to envision the new!

IN RECENT DECADES WE HAVE SEEN A LOT OF DRESSING DOWN: CASUAL FRIDAYS, LESS BODY COVERAGE, WEARING COLOURFUL CLOTHES TO FUNERALS: ARE WE WITNESSING THE END OF THE DRESS CODE?

I don't think we will get rid of dress codes. But they might become less and less prescriptive. Clothing will always be an expression of self and how we relate to others – our role in society, in private and professional environments. Even if wearing black to a funeral is no longer a necessity, it is still generally accepted. To wear white at a wedding unless you are the bride remains a faux pas. Especially at work where a uniform or protective clothing is required, clothing traditions have been largely resistant to the de-formalisation that we have seen with office dress codes.

BUT IF WE LOOK AT MODERN WORKING ENVIRONMENTS, THE "SUIT" HAS BECOME LESS COMPULSORY.

Yes. But even though we saw a steady casualisation of clothes at work, this has mainly been true for small companies with flat hierarchies, such as start-ups. Or, of course, for the increasing mass of people who work from home. In bigger enterprises this is less so. Throughout history, there have always been hierarchies: people who are in charge and others, who follow their instructions. This will remain – and will be expressed in the way we dress ourselves. Moreover, in dangerous jobs, for example in the laboratory or on the construction site, working clothes will continue to have a protective function. Displaying professionalism is another function of the dress code in the working environment. Therefore, the tradition that doctors and dentists are dressed in white coats is unlikely to be entirely abandoned in the near future. And if it is, it will be replaced by another sort of professional uniform. Even increasing heterogenization of society won't put a total stop to the dress code. Each group will have their own, slightly altered dress codes. Conventions will remain, even within smaller groups – maybe even more so to distance themselves from other communities.

IN THE PAST DECADES WE HAVE SEEN A TREND FOR VINTAGE CLOTHING. IS THIS A REACTION TO INCREASING AUTOMATION?

In the 1990s, at the turn of the millennium, we began to see the proliferation of fast fashion, and the emergence of vintage style. The two go hand in hand. When you reach the point in manufacturing and economics where everybody can afford to dress on trend, what do we do as humans, who are always looking for some kind of distinction? We start to search for second-hand clothing, for something, ideally, no one else has. In a world of mass market uniformity, this search for something unique will become ever more important as a powerful way to express our personality. And wearing vintage does not only make us appear different – but skilled: being able to find this unique piece of dress or jewellery qualifies us as experts in the field. It can be compared with one's music or book collection: We take pride in a collection that is not made for us by others, but put together ourselves.

WITH FAST-CHANGING FASHION AND A VARIETY OF STYLES IN MIND: WHAT HAPPY PAST WILL WE RELATE TO TOMORROW?

As we look back, each generation's specific looks and trends will become clear, even if it was marked by various styles. There will be things that are typical of our time, that come to define a decade. This sometimes only becomes visible in retrospect. For example, the 1990s were quite heterogeneous in style. We had grunge, minimalism and bodycon styles. And today all of these styles are sought after and considered to define the Nineties.

The space age costumes of the science fiction films of the 1960s still affect the way we imagine the future of clothing today: Jane Fonda in "Barbarella", 1968.

Today it might be the simple white sneaker, associated with Phoebe Philo, and the current trend for modest dressing which has crossed into secular life, as well as being a feature of religious dress for some communities. High necklines, wide cuts and loose clothing are all styles we may associate with the 2010s, which also ties in to ideas around gender neutrality. Athleisure and the continued rise of sportswear is another example.

WILL HANDCRAFTED GOODS ALSO BENEFIT FROM THIS NOSTALGIA?

Yes, but not only due to our love for the old and its methods of production. This will be the luxury of tomorrow! Now that made-to-measure can be produced by machines, it's becoming less exclusive. As a result, the idea of handcrafted clothing becomes more desirable. Handcrafted techniques, like embroidery, will be what we consider as true luxury.

IN YOUR OPINION: WHAT WILL REMAIN THE SAME IN THE FUTURE OF CLOTHING?

The meaning of clothing will change, but it will always have a cultural meaning. Clothing will never be a blank flag. It is too bound up with identity, with the way we present ourselves to the world. So the meaning will change but there will always be meaning there.

WHAT IS YOUR PERSONAL VISION OF THE FUTURE OF CLOTHING?

I believe that the medicalization of clothing has huge potential. To be able to wear clothes that can help us to remain healthy is a great concept. Along with sustainability. So my ideal garment is something that looks amazing, is not destroying the planet and can improve or monitor our health. I believe this should be possible in the not-too-distant future.

AMBER BUTCHART
is a fashion historian, author and broadcaster who specialises in the historical intersections between dress, politics and culture. She was the presenter of BBC4's six-part series "A Stitch in Time" that fused biography and art to explore the lives of historical figures through the clothes they wore. She is an Associate Lecturer at London College of Fashion, a former Research Fellow at University of the Arts London, and has written five books on the history and culture of dress.

SUSTAINABILITY AND FUNCTION

THE REDISCOVERY OF TRUE NEEDS

DAVID DE ROTHSCHILD

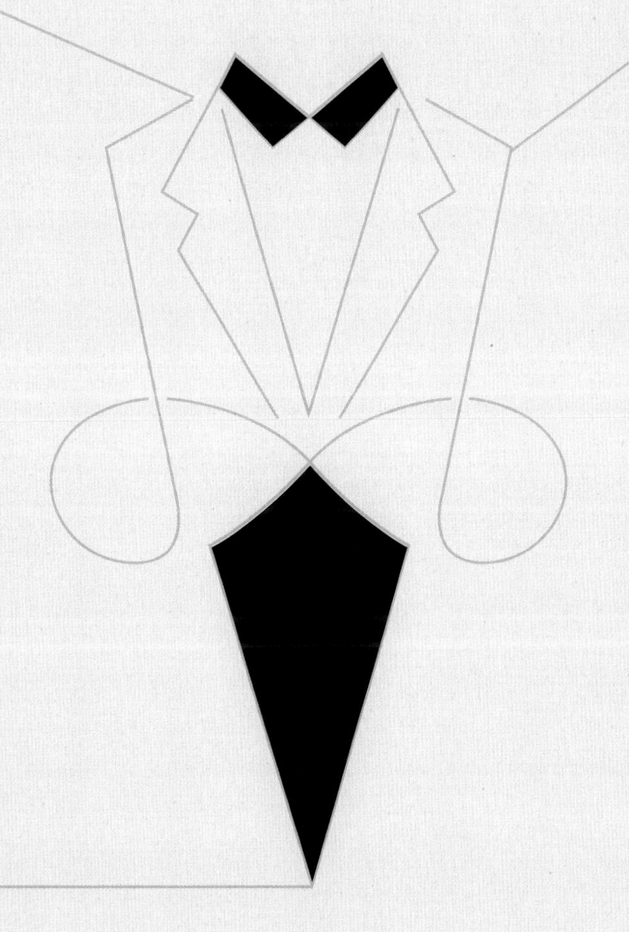

There is no such thing as sustainable clothing, there is only sustainable behaviour. What we wear, how much we buy and how we treat our belongings, claims the adventurer and environmentalist David de Rothschild. Nevertheless, the fusion of garment and technology could make clothing more ecological in the long run. And might even bring us back in touch with our senses.

HOW IMPORTANT ARE CLOTHES FOR YOU?

What matters to me is less the final product – the garment itself – than the material it is made of. I believe there is a certain energy to material. If something is made well and sustainably produced, you can feel it. Clothes that are synthetic and of poor quality can hardly be healthy in the long run.

CAN YOU EXPLAIN?

Think about it: We spend so much time in our clothes all our life long. It is the closest thing that touches our body every day. We tend to forget that our skin is our largest organ. It is the front line, the fence between us and the external environment. And it is smart: It can self-heal, breathe, regulate temperature and fend off bacteria through protective barriers. Whatever you put on to your skin should not hinder the body's function. So we should choose well what kind of "second skin" we wear.

TALKING OF SECOND SKIN: COULD CLOTHES IN THE FUTURE NOT ONLY ALLOW OUR SKIN TO FUNCTION BUT ALSO AUGMENT ITS ABILITIES?

Yes. I believe that we are moving into an age in which your bodily functions and clothes are becoming one and the same. We are, however, at a very early stage in this development. So far we have only managed to attach external devices like cell phones or fitness trackers to our bodies. In a few years time, technology will be much more integrated: function and form will be connected; the sensors will be in the fabric, monitoring and controlling our health. Do I welcome this development? Well, it can certainly make life easy, especially for the chronically ill, who are informed of a sudden rise in blood pressure or reminded to take their pills. At the moment, a fabric is being tested that can deploy the right dosage of medicine throughout the day which could reduce the risk of false therapy.

AND WHAT ARE THE DOWNSIDES OF TECHNOLOGICAL GARMENTS?

It is quite ironic: By becoming more digitised, we are becoming more disconnected from our body, as we create so much noise and distraction. I was far off in Norway without any digital devices and the one thing I noticed most was the silence. Suddenly I heard a noise: the blood running inside my body. Today we need to incorporate devices in our lives to tell us that we are hot or cold, even though our skin provides us with all necessary information and reacts accordingly: the pores open to sweat when we are hot, when we are cold we get goosebumps to retain the heat. Also, when we get really cold and our temperature drops, the body acts what we call smart today: it prioritises. What is more important, a toe or a liver? And it starts to move warm blood to the important parts.

The human focus on technology is driven by the idea that it will make us smarter, whereas it leaves as more detached and – as a result – less intelligent. Technology alienated us from our bodies, but the next generation of wearables could also be the way back to our senses.

WHAT OTHER FUNCTIONS COULD CLOTHES HAVE IN THE FUTURE?

They will not only control our health but protect us from illnesses. I believe that biomimicry – the copying of nature's smartness – could play a vital role in the future of clothing and its fusion with the health sector. One example is shark skin. The skin of sharks has a certain pattern that bacteria does not like to grow on. There is a company in Germany, called Sharklet, that imitates that pattern and uses it for door handles in hotel rooms as well as cell phone screens. Imagine if we created a glove, like a second skin, that we could put on our fingers, invisible or fashionable, that would stop us from picking up bacteria!

TALKING OF NEW MATERIALS IN THE CONTEXT OF SUSTAINABILITY: WHAT NEW OR OLD FABRIC WILL PLAY A ROLE IN THE FASHION BUSINESS?

Fashion is a 3 trillion dollar business and the world's second largest polluter after oil. Material plays a major role in this. The most important is cotton, from which 40 percentage of our clothing is made. Even though it is a natural fibre it is probably the most water intensive and it makes up over 10 percent of the worldwide pesticides market. The second largest fabric is polyester, which is highly dependent on oil and its

"We have to make things again that last. And get rid of seasons."

DAVID DE ROTHSCHILD

Biomimicry could play a vital role in the fusion of clothing with the health sector: Here we see a 3D rendering of a sharkskin imitating wound dressing. The structure is supposed to speed up the healing process by promoting cellular migration.

Picture: © Eye of Science

microfibres, when washed, are starting to come away from the fabric and go into the water supply. In the long run, we need to substitute these materials, at least partly. One new material that will play a role is artificially produced spider silk. Spider silk is five times stronger than steel of the same diameter. It is the toughest natural fibre known and we will soon start to see it move from the laboratory into the factory. Spider silk clothing can be a replacement for synthetics like nylon and polyester, and is already been used for making jewellery due to its robustness.

Model Bianca posing in a cape made from the golden silk of 1.2 million spiders at Victoria & Albert Museum on January 23, 2012 in London, England.

Photo by Fred Duval/WireImage, Courtesy of Getty Images

WHAT ARE OTHER WAYS TO MAKE THE CLOTHING BUSINESS MORE SUSTAINABLE?

The main challenge is to remove the design aspect and focus on quality. We have to make things again that last. And get rid of seasons! Fashion is creating needs that we don't have. This season everyone is wearing pink, so I need pink. That is a false need and it has to be addressed.

HOW CAN WE CHANGE PEOPLE'S ATTITUDE?

It is a slow process of rising awareness on the side of the clients and of changing the business models of the companies on the other side. The two will reinforce each other. As companies and brands become more important for people's lives, they have greater responsibility to collaborate and to communicate. Transparency is greater now, with social networks, and that responsibility will be exposed if it is not used correctly. We have so many devices today to get informed about supply chains, manufacturing and distribution processes – you can't hide with your brand. And we have so much more choice now. You have to pay attention otherwise people move.

DO YOU BELIEVE THAT THE NEXT GENERATION OF CUSTOMERS WILL BUY FROM COMPANIES THAT ARE MORE SUSTAINABLE?

Yes, I do. People want to identify with the products they wear. And sustainability will be one important criterion. Our relationship with nature and the planet is much more part of the system, of the education, than when I was a child. People want their attitude to be reflected. However, things are celebrated for being sustainable that are not. For example, a few years ago, a company was given an award for producing a wrap for bananas out of bioplastic. Biopackaging on a banana is absurd – it already has the best packaging in the world. Its intelligent skin protects the fruit and indicates its readiness to be eaten.

UNDER THE LABEL "THE LOST EXPLORER" YOU ARE SELLING "UNIVERSAL" CLOTHES. CAN YOU TELL US MORE ABOUT THIS PROJECT?

The idea was to create a universal wardrobe, in which you can travel, dine and dance, have meetings and camp. Our clothes are made to fit the various environments we linger – from natural ones like a desert, mountain and the sea to cities, streets and meeting rooms. The "Magic Jacket", for example, looks like a classic veston [short coat], yet is made of water-repellent material and has several pockets.

However, "The Lost Explorer" is not sustainable in itself. Only behaviour can be sustainable: What you buy with your money, how you treat it, what choices you make. Our clothes also leave a footprint during production, distributing and sending them back and forth – if they don't please the customer. Some people buy the same garment in three different colours. That is buying a good conscience not a change in behaviour. Nevertheless: "Sustainable products" start to shift the conversation.

YET NOT EVERYBODY CAN BUY GOOD QUALITY CLOTHING.

I don't really agree. We create false markets. People believe they get more than they used to. In many ways this is wrong. Just because you can buy a shirt for 7 dollars does not mean you are better off. Back in the day people owned fewer clothes, but they lasted half a lifetime – and could be mended. Nowadays garments are intentionally made to fall apart after some months. So you end up spending more money on less instead of buying less but of good quality.

WHAT IS YOUR PREFERRED GARMENT?

A handkerchief. It is the best and simplest example of style and function.

DAVID DE ROTHSCHILD
is a British adventurer and ecologist and head of the Sculpt the Future Foundation, a charity that supports innovations and creativity in social and environmental impact efforts. A member of the English banking family, the Rothschilds, he studied Political Science and Information Systems in Oxford and natural medicine in London. In 2010, he became famous for crossing the Pacific in a catamaran made of plastic bottles and recycled materials to draw attention to marine pollution. Recently, he has founded the sustainable clothing brand "The Lost Explorer", which focuses on the development of a universal wardrobe, in which people should be able to dine, dance and go to work.

CRAFTSMANSHIP AND SKILLS

MATERIAL IS THE MOTHER OF INVENTION

RICHARD SENNETT

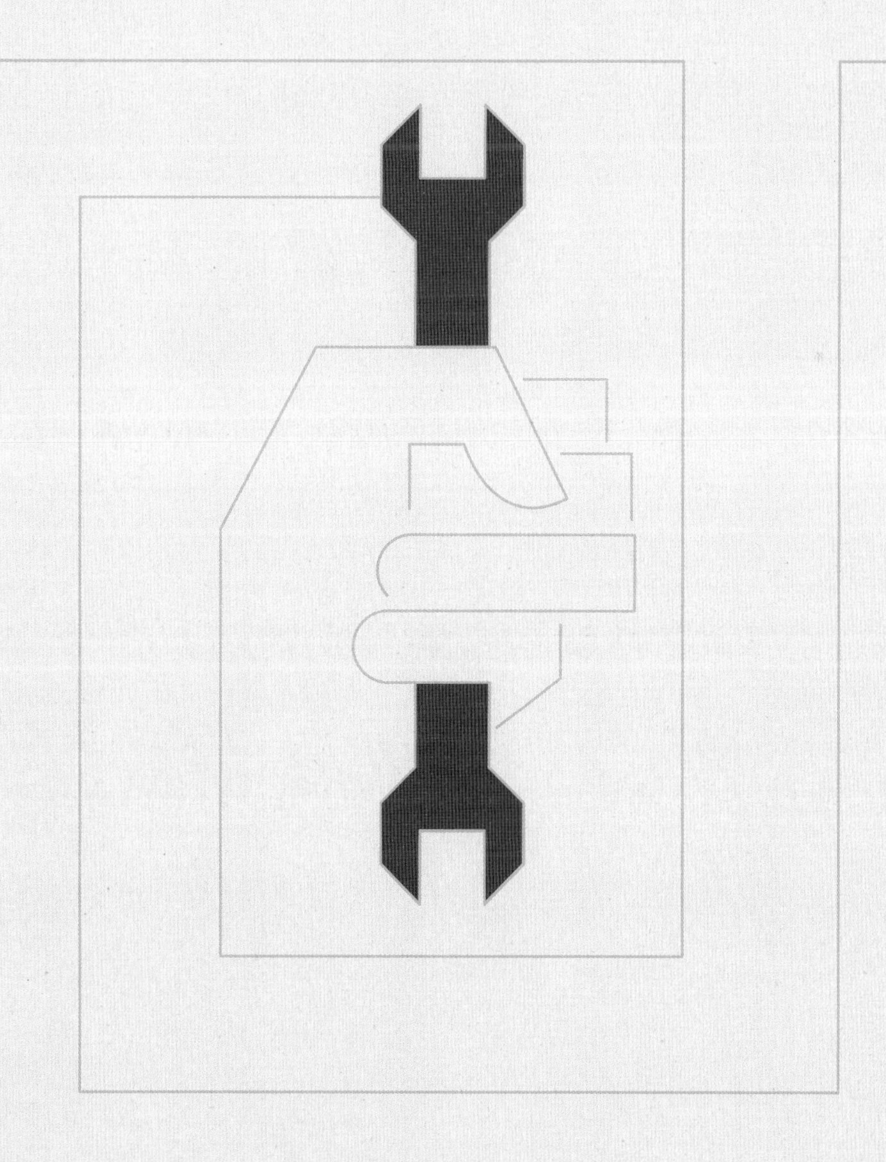

Handcrafted clothes will become more important in the future. Not only will people start to reject poor quality but they will value the making process – particularly in times of automation, says Richard Sennett. The sociologist and author of *The Craftsman* praises the learning effects of working with material and tells us how to remain the masters of our own products.

WITH *THE CRAFTSMAN* YOU PUBLISHED A HOMAGE TO HANDICRAFT IN A TIME OF AUTOMATION. WHY?

The Craftsman is not mainly engaged with physical work, but with how we get good quality of work in a very general sense. And interestingly, the ingredients for good work are the same today as they used to be for the weaver some hundred years ago: years of training and learning different ways to deal with and understand the "material" we work with – any type of material. It does not matter if it is wool, food, computers, other people or our natural environment.

SO THERE IS NO DIFFERENCE BETWEEN PHYSICAL WORK AND KNOWLEDGE WORK?

Yes and no. On the one hand, we all deal with material. Whether it is tangible or not is not so important for the quality of the work that emerges from it. On the other hand, physical work, unlike knowledge work, forces us to deal with the material we work with in a more active way.

"It is easier to make a tailor into a computer programmer than the other way round."

RICHARD SENNETT

Doing physical work means entering a dialogue with resistance. Materials don't always do what we want them to; machines are faulty. This dialogue of the maker with the tools and the material is a constant process of learning, of trying out new and better ways to handle our environment. Computer programmers are people who learnt to do just one technical job. This is executing, not crafting – a major difference. Non-physical labour often has little learning effect. Craftspeople, however, are forced to be experimental and to continuously think critically about the working process. That's why it is easier to turn a tailor into a computer programmer than the other way round.

SHOULD SCHOOLS AND UNIVERSITIES FIRST TEACH US HOW TO KNIT AND STITCH BEFORE WE BECOME BANKERS OR PROFESSORS?

Yes. Education should provide young people with the opportunity to make as much material experience as possible. Physical work makes us innovative as we are continuously dealing with incompleteness. Aware of the fact that the end product will not be perfect we still try to find ways to improve it.

Crafting has been rediscovered as a potent way to understand the old and new materials and objects that surround us. DIY Gamer Kit designed by Technology Will Save US.

IN THE FEW YEARS SINCE *THE CRAFTSMAN* WAS PUBLISHED "MAKING THINGS" HAS BECOME A NEW TREND. WHAT DO YOU THINK OF THAT DEVELOPMENT?

I did not write the book to start the maker-movement and I don't know too much about it. But we share a common wish: to get better quality. When it comes to consumer products, this means less mass fabrication and more individuality. I think this is especially necessary in the field of eating – our most basic need. As a result of mass production, taste and healthiness of food have declined and it is vital that something as important as food should be of better quality in the future. It is also necessary with clothes: what we put on should not harm our health or that of the environment. And it should last for more than a couple of weeks. The making movement is not nostalgic, as some people discount it as, but it is the refusal to consume poor products.

TALKING OF CLOTHES: NOT EVERYBODY HAS THE TIME – OR THE ABILITY – TO DESIGN OR KNIT A JUMPER. WILL 3D PRINTERS ALLOW MORE PEOPLE TO BECOME DESIGNERS OF THEIR OWN CLOTHES?

That depends on whether we have the control over the printer, the machine. It is not necessary that we do things with our bare hands. What makes the feeling of selfmade is to have the responsibility over the tools that help us to make something – whether this is a printer or a hammer. If we only need to push the button and have no influence on the design or the program that prints the jumper, then we are neither craftspeople nor designers and our products are not of better quality than those made in factories.

YOU DEFINE CRAFTSMANSHIP AS “THE DESIRE TO DO A GOOD JOB AS AN END IN ITSELF”. WHAT CAN WE DO AS INDIVIDUALS TO BECOME GOOD CRAFTSPEOPLE?

We need to learn to treat a computer as a tool the way the carpenter does the chisel. And fortunately the technological progress is helping us to get there. Let’s take computer programs as an example. Until recently, they were easy to use without thinking. In the future, they will be replaced by self-programming. A second computer age is about to begin, in which it will be possible to use modern tools like traditional ones, as they allow us to influence the end product. Mass-produced things, on which the buyer has no influence – whether programs or clothes – will soon belong to the past, I believe. And I am happy about that.

RICHARD SENNETT

is a US sociologist. He teaches at New York University and at the London School of Economics and Political Science. His main research fields are cities, labour and cultural sociology. In his book *The Craftsman* (2008), he calls for the restoration of the intrinsic value of individual labour and for working conditions to be designed in such a way that people will want to do their work as well as possible. Sennett is married to urban sociologist Saskia Sassen.

FUNCTIONALISATION AND TECHNOLOGY

INTERFACING THE BODY

LINH LE

In the near future, clothes will do more than keep us warm and make us look nice, Linh Le, the CEO of the smart textile start-up Bonbouton, is convinced. They will connect our body to the outside world and shield it from invisible harms. Yet this will only come about if they can be designed to look like ordinary garments and they can be kept updated.

WHAT WILL WE BE WEARING IN THE FUTURE?

We will still wear clothes! And they might not look that much different from the ones we are wearing today. However, their function will change. One of the main purposes of clothes has always been to provide protection from the natural environment, such as heat and cold. In the future, clothing will be able to do much more than that. It will be interfacing the body with the outside world. On the one hand, from the inside to the outside: Smart clothing will be able to analyse our body reactions, such as sweat or changing heartbeat, and "transport" this information to the surface so that we can, if necessary, address any problem. On the other hand, smart clothing will shield us from the outside to the inside, but in a much more elaborate way than today, taking into consideration new risks, such as smog or radiation. In this way, smart clothes function as an alarm system that augment our senses: if our eyes and nose do not pick up these invisible risks, clothes will have to do it for us. In a second phase, our clothes will hopefully not only detect the source of harm, but also immediately protect us from it, for example, by putting some sort of shield or filter around us.

WITH THESE VISIONS IN MIND: DO WE NEED TO REDEFINE CLOTHING?

We will definitely redefine the role of clothing. Clothes in the future will have various interfacing functions, depending on what capabilities we add, from reactive tasks like collecting information, to pro-active tasks like providing warmth or sending out alarm signals. Some people will have a multitude of functional clothing, each with a specific use. Others will combine several functions in one suit or dress which accompanies them in every life situation. In either case, clothes will become more important.

IF "INTERFACING" US IS THE NEW FUNCTION OF CLOTHING: WILL IT ALSO PLAY A LEADING ROLE IN THE CONTROL OF OUR SMART ENVIRONMENT?

Yes, I believe so. First, it is only a matter of time until we are able to fully integrate technological gadgets into clothing. So it is very likely that the smart phone will be replaced by smart clothing – and eventually cease to exist. Second, our clothing, like a second self, will be a means to identify oneself to other people and to our intelligent environment. It will be simple and safe to shop online and pay bills with our clothes. Or to automatically open doors from a distance with a touch on the sleeve.

REALITY CHECK: TODAY, SMART CLOTHING IS STILL A SMALL NICHE. DO YOU BELIEVE THE FUTURE OF CLOTHING IS SMART?

Today, smart clothing is highly dependent on special materials in which the technological gadgets can be integrated. Tomorrow, however, it should be fabric-independent. To achieve this, we will have to integrate tiny sensors into the fibre before making the garment. The long-term vision is to mix this smart fibre with normal fibre and get any piece of garment you like with any mode of production. Mass-production or bespoke tailoring – any segment could use smart fabric. And the customer still has the choice to wear any sort of material – from natural cotton, to synthetic polymer – with all the advantages of modern technology. Once "smart clothes" is replaced by "smart fabric", which is no longer forced to integrate whole gadgets into the clothing, then, yes: The future of clothing will be smart.

SO EVERYONE WILL WEAR FUNCTIONAL CLOTHES?

I believe so. But it will happen in several stages. The first stage of adoption is happening right now with elite athletes who seek to improve their professional performance. The next group of adoption could come from chronically ill and elderly people taking advantage of medical applications with specific uses. And eventually, the general audience will start picking up.

It is likely that clothes and accessories will no longer only protect us from the outside but will also interact with it: The "SEIL-bag" illustrates traffic signals such as cruise, stop and the emergency signal on the bicycle rider's backpack.

“It is very likely that the smart phone will be replaced by smart clothing.”

LINH LE

IS THIS THE END OF FAST FASHION AS GARMENTS WILL BE MORE EXPENSIVE IN THE FUTURE?

At the moment smart clothing is a premium product, as it is still very expensive to produce. But with increasing technological progress it will become cheaper. Take the smart phone as an example: 20 years ago most people could not afford to buy one, today everybody has them. I believe the same will happen with smart clothes or textiles. In the next ten or fifteen years, innovation and increasing acceptance will have made them affordable for the mass. As a consequence, we will not call them smart clothes in the future: Just clothes. And the garments we wear today might be called “stupid clothes”.

EVEN IF THEY BECOME AFFORDABLE: ARE "THE NEW CLOTHES" A WAY TO MAKE CLOTHING MORE SUSTAINABLE - AS WE KEEP THEM LONGER?

That will depend on people's attitude – and it should stay that way. People need to be able to decide if they want to get rid of their clothes or keep them. Especially the latter will be a challenge to functional clothes: they can become outdated; lose their function, something that cannot happen to ordinary garments. For me, in terms of phones, the iPhone 5 is good enough. And I want to be given an option to keep it in the future. The same should apply for clothes.

For this reason it is vital that one focus of the invention around smart clothing is on how to make them durable. Meaning: Batteries will have to be easily replaced and apps updated. For this purpose, batteries probably have to stay outside the fibre – unlike everything else – so that we can easily exchange it.

AND HOW CAN WE DISPOSE OF THEM - AS THEY ARE GADGET AND GARMENT?

If we manage to update our functional clothing, we might keep them for a lifetime. If we still want to get rid of them, however, the best thing is to recycle them. For this purpose an efficient recycling process has to be developed, that disassembles the various components of clothes and reuses them – for technology only or for new functional garments.

IF WE THINK OF SMART CLOTHING NOT ONLY AS A RANDOM PHENOMENON BUT AS A LASTING AND WIDESPREAD DEVELOPMENT: HOW HEALTHY IS AN HOURLY CONTROL OF ONE'S OWN HEALTH?

There is a fine line between controlling and over-controlling. We will have to learn not to do the latter. It can be compared to the use of the smart phone. It is our decision how often we check the updates. And, of course, it depends on the technology, which should provide the user with the "right amount" of monitoring. For example, medical applications usually require both more hours for monitoring and a higher level of intrusiveness, compared to other consumer applications. However, in terms of health, it is proven to be best to take the preventive approach compared to a last minute cure. And the most effective way to prevent illness or poor health is to collect enough historical data of the user. There are, of course, many risks associated with being controlled or monitored all the time and of data being used inappropriately. This is a challenge we will have to deal with – with or without the existence of smart clothes.

LINH LE is the CEO of the smart clothing start-up Bonbouton. The New York City-based team of innovators specialises in inkjet-printed, low-cost graphene solutions. With technology licensed from the Stevens Institute of Technology, the company has emerged as an industry leader in microsensor technology, developing mechanically flexible and molecularly thin sensors for monitoring skin temperature and structure with graphene oxide (GO). Bonbouton's first product is a smart insole, which passively monitors the skin's physiological signals in order to detect early signs of foot ulcers. Linh Le, who holds a PhD in Chemical Engineering, has the long-term vision to bring "cutting-edge sensing technology into one of the most human essentials, clothes".

“Taste is nothing more than fashion.”

SALVADOR DALÍ

A SHOE FOR MERCURY COMPLETE WITH SPRINGBACK HEELS SO THAT HE CAN WALK LIKE AN ANGEL

CYBERNETIC GENTLEMAN WITH CASSETTE DRAWERS IN WHICH THE ENTIRE HISTORY OF CIVILISATION IS RECORDED ON MICRO-FILM

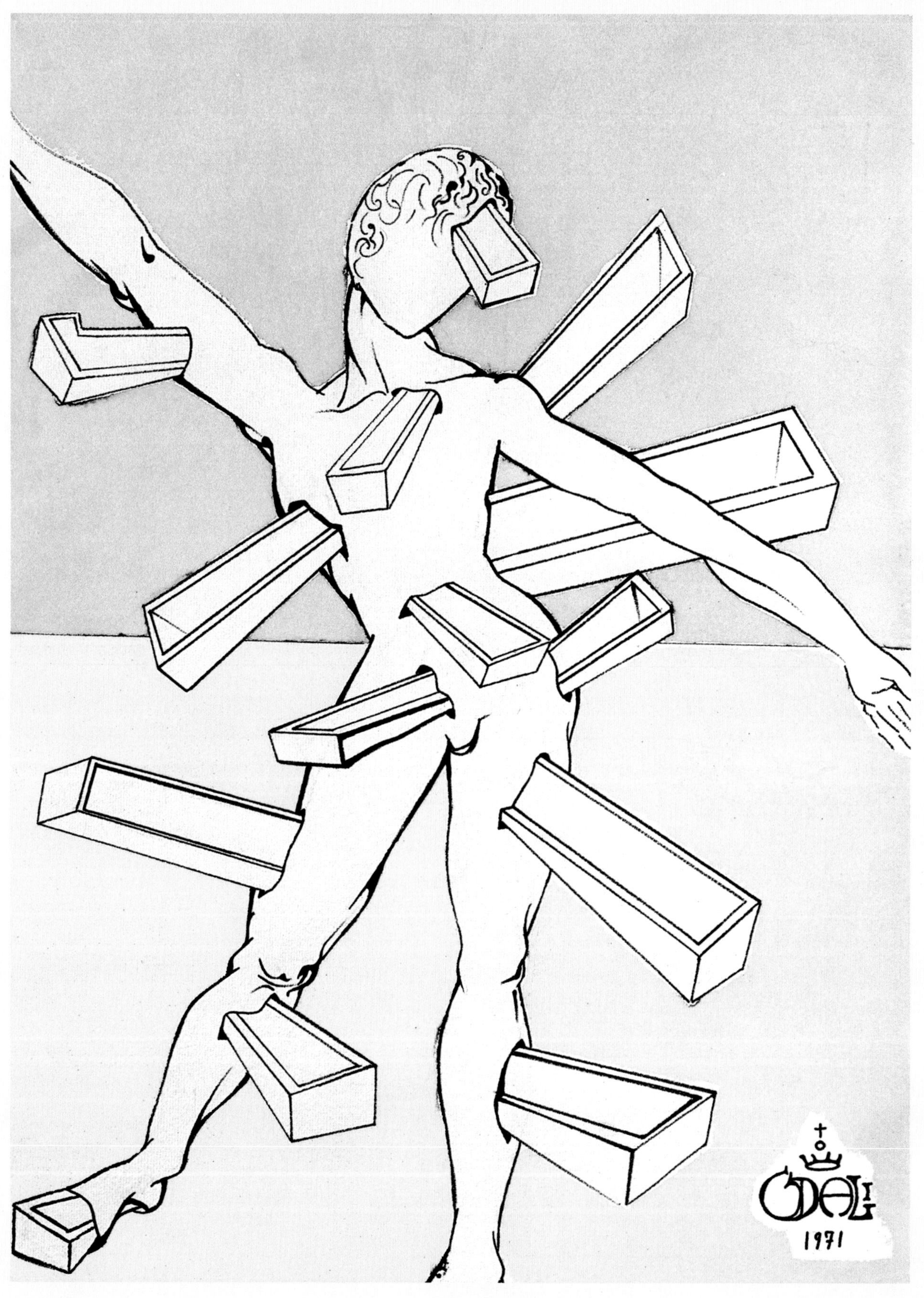

“Dress influences behaviour as much as appearance.”

SALVADOR DALÍ

CLOTHES WILL CHANGE. THE HUMAN BODY, TOO!

YUVAL HARARI

To know what we will be wearing in the future requires an understanding of what we will be. And in this respect, we are facing the most fundamental change in human history, says Yuval Harari, historian and author of *Sapiens: A Brief History of Humankind* (2015). Not only the modes of production will be reshaped, but also the human body. The keys to success will remain the same, however: believe in your ideology but adapt to change. For example: dressing robots and cyborgs, instead of humans. Now take a look into the future of humanity!

WHAT ARE, IN YOUR OPINION, THE BIGGEST CHALLENGES TO THE LONGEVITY OF OUR SOCIETY?

The greatest challenge at present is the breath-taking pace of technological development. Twenty-five years ago, there was no Internet; look at where we are today. Institutions, governments and legal codes and individuals are not built to withstand such rapid changes. And the pace is only increasing. In the middle of the 19th century, when faced by the Industrial Revolution, Karl Marx said "all that is solid melts into air". This is doubly true today. Nobody has any idea what the world will look like in 30–40 years. For example, we don't know how the job market will look: When computer algorithms outperform humans in more and more cognitive tasks, will most people still have jobs? Will most humans still be useful for anything? Similarly, we don't know what advances in biotechnology will do to human sexuality, human identity or family structure. What will society look like when, for the first time in history, the rich will be biologically different from the poor, and 80 will be the new 40?

NEVERTHELESS, SOCIETIES HAVE PROVEN SURPRISINGLY RESILIENT TO MASSIVE CHANGE AND DAMAGE, TAKE EUROPE AND THE TWO WORLD WARS FOR EXAMPLE. DO YOU BELIEVE THAT THE CHANGES WE ARE FACING TODAY ARE EVEN MORE FUNDAMENTAL, MEANING THERE IS NO WAY BACK TO THE WORLD WE KNOW?

It seems we are witnessing the most fundamental change in human history. The old economic and political system is becoming irrelevant. And there is no going back. Throughout history there have been many economic, social and political revolutions. But one thing has remained constant: humanity itself. We still have the same body and mind as our ancestors in the Roman Empire or ancient Egypt. Yet in the coming decades, for the first time in history, humanity itself will undergo a radical revolution. Not only our society and economy, but our bodies and minds will be transformed by genetic engineering, nanotechnology and brain-computer interfaces. In such a world, the old structures will become completely obsolete, and society will have to create new structures.

HOW MUCH CHANGE CAN WE TOLERATE TO BE ABLE TO LAST? AND WHEN WILL IT TRIGGER COLLAPSE?

Modern society is built on change. It expects change, and even demands it. Change has become the only constant. We don't know what the future will look like, but we know and expect the world will be completely different from what it is today. Hence our society is surprisingly resilient in the face of change. The one thing certain to trigger collapse is the absence of change, the absence of economic growth, the absence of new technological inventions.

LET'S TAKE THE CURRENT ECONOMIC CRISES: ARE WE AT A TIPPING POINT OF CAPITALISM?

Capitalism has many faults, but at present we don't know of any viable alternative. The last serious alternative – communism – discredited itself so thoroughly that few people have the stomach to try again. I think the main challenge for anyone who dislikes capitalism is to formulate a realistic alternative. And it is high time we came up with something, because capitalism indeed seems to be heading towards a major crisis. I think the main economic problem we will face in the 21st century is what to do with all the "useless" people. Computer algorithms are catching up with humans in more and more cognitive fields. It is extremely unlikely that computers will develop anything even close to human consciousness, but in order to replace humans in the economy, computers don't need consciousness. They just need intelligence.

CAN YOU EXPLAIN?

Throughout history, intelligence always went hand in hand with consciousness. The only intelligent entities were conscious entities. The only ones who could play chess, drive vehicles, fight wars and diagnose diseases were conscious – aware – human beings. But intelligence is now decoupling from consciousness. We are developing non-conscious algorithms that can play chess, drive vehicles, fight wars and diagnose diseases better than us. When the economy has to choose between intelligence and consciousness, the economy will choose intelligence. It has no real need for consciousness. Once self-driving cars and doctor-bots outperform human drivers and doctors, millions of drivers and doctors around the world will lose their jobs, even though self-driving cars and doctor-bots are not conscious. What will be the use of humans in such a world? What will we do with billions of economically useless humans? We don't know. We don't have any economic model for such a situation.

DO WE KNOW WHICH INDUSTRIES WILL STILL BE RELEVANT IN THE FUTURE?

Up until now, humans have mastered the production of things: of vehicles, weapons, tools, textiles, foodstuffs. In the next phase of history, we will master the production of ourselves. We will use biotechnology and computers to engineer and produce bodies and minds. The main industries will, accordingly, involve the engineering and production of bodies and minds. But as noted earlier, it is far from certain that these industries will offer many jobs for humans.

"The most amazing thing about the future won't be the spaceships, but the beings flying them."

YUVAL HARARI

AS PREDICTING THE FUTURE IS BECOMING EVER MORE DIFFICULT: DOES IT STILL MAKE SENSE TO DEFINE LONG-TERM STRATEGIES OR DO WE MAINLY NEED THE ABILITY TO REACT TO SHORT-TERM CHANGE?

Precisely because we cannot predict the future, we need long-term strategies. Otherwise, we will just be pushed hither and thither by the currents of history. Unfortunately, it seems that politicians are giving up on the future. For much of the twentieth century political parties had all-encompassing visions about the future of humankind. You had communist, fascist and liberal visions competing against each other. Today, no political party has any vision to speak of. Politicians have become administrators rather than leaders or visionaries, and almost all political debates concern short-term tactical disagreements, rather than strategic dilemmas. The only ones thinking seriously about the future of humankind are business entrepreneurs, such as the people running Google or Apple. Who, today, are the equivalents of Lenin or Mao, who sought to destroy an old world and build a completely new world in its stead? Sergey Brin and Mark Zuckerberg. Not that their visions are ruthless and murderous like those of Lenin or Mao. I have absolutely no intention of making such a comparison. I am comparing the visions only in terms of their boldness and magnitude: the boldness to aim at reengineering the entire world, and build a new human society from scratch.

SO WOULD YOU SAY THAT BELIEVING IN A BOLD IDEA IS ONE OF THE KEYS TO ENSURING THE FUTURE OF INSTITUTIONS OR EVEN NATIONS?

Yes. First you need to believe in your ideology. Doubletalk and deceit work well only in the short term. Institutions such as the Catholic Church or the United States survived successfully for so many centuries because most of the people who led and served them really believed in their ideals. The Soviet Union collapsed because by the 1980s, not even its ruling caste believed in it. Secondly, you need to be flexible, and adapt to change. The Catholic Church has reinvented itself so many times over the last two millennia. If it wants to survive into the third millennium, it will have to reinvent itself again. These two strategies are somewhat contradictory. How to reinvent yourself without giving up on your core ideals? Those who cannot perform this delicate dance cannot survive. Either they hold on to outdated forms – and collapse; or they give up their core values – and dissolve.

YOU SAID ONCE THAT THE MOST IMPORTANT THINGS IN THE WORLD ONLY EXIST IN OUR IMAGINATION. HOW DO WE NEED TO RE-IMAGINE OUR SOCIETY?

We certainly need new fictions, new mythologies, new religions. And these are being created at this very moment in places such as Silicon Valley. The most interesting place today from a religious perspective is not the Middle East, but Silicon Valley. The engineers at Google, Facebook, Apple and Microsoft are creating far more than just devices and algorithms. They are creating the next wave of universal religions. Techno-religions that make all the old promises – happiness, justice, prosperity, paradise – but here on Earth with the help of technology rather than after death with the help of supernatural beings. Yet at the same time we also need to beware of fictions, and to reconnect to reality. We are living in a world comprised of fictional stories about gods, nations, human rights, money and corporations. Modern society cannot function without the help of these fictions. But we are paying a very high price for losing touch with the real world: the world of sensations, bodies, animals, trees, rocks. Over the last two

"Precisely because we cannot predict the future, we need longterm strategies."

YUVAL HARARI

centuries, humans have increasingly lost the ability to live in the here and now, to be aware of their sensations and of the immediate world surrounding them. We increasingly live in a virtual reality of our own making. This has given us immense new powers, but it has also made us strangers to ourselves, and more alienated than ever before. So we are very powerful, but not very happy.

DO YOU HAVE ONE PIECE OF ADVICE ON HOW TO BECOME HAPPIER IN THE FUTURE?

I think the oldest advice is the best, and it is applicable to all: know thyself. We are going to face enormous new opportunities and enormous new dangers. The biggest problem of all is that we will have unprecedented power, including the power to change ourselves and our very bodies and minds, but we don't know what to do with this power. For that, we need to know who we are and what we really want. And most people don't know that. Throughout history, humans have shown a remarkable ability to acquire power, but they have been far less successful in translating power into happiness. But how to know thyself? I would start with body sensations. Over the last two centuries, humans have become increasingly disembodied beings, living apart and away from their bodies. This process has been accelerating over the last two decades as a result of the information revolution. We are connecting ourselves to a virtual world of information, while disconnecting from our immediate sensory world. If we want to know who we are, I would start by learning the value of silence, of being just here and now, and of paying close attention to what I am actually sensing right here, right now.

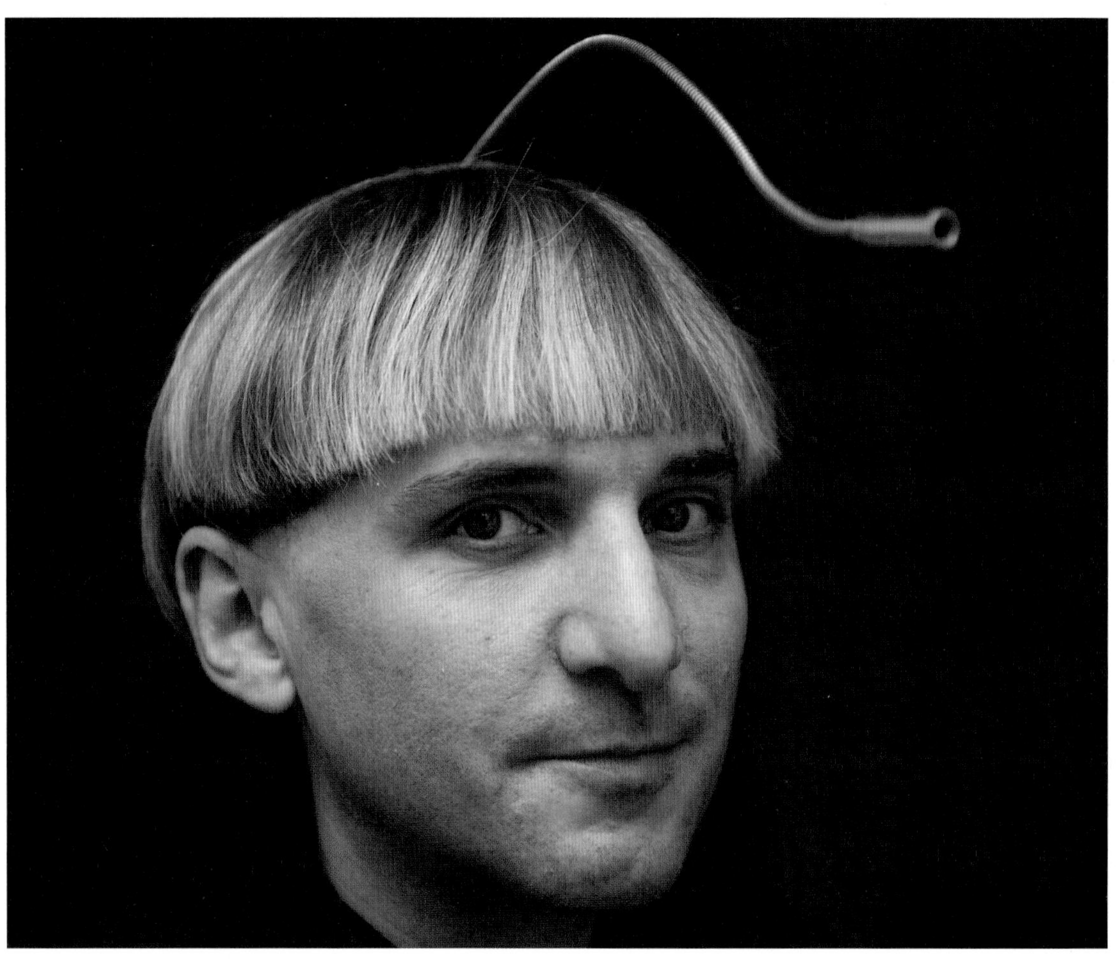

The wearers of tomorrow's clothes will not only be human: Neil Harbisson, cyborg artist and activist, the first person legally recognised as a cyborg by a government and first person with an antenna implanted in his skull to extend his senses.

YOU CLAIM THAT "HUMANS HAVE PASSED THEIR EXPIRY DATE". COULD YOU EXPLAIN? FOR HOW LONG AND IN WHAT FORM ARE WE GOING TO EXIST?

Humans evolved in adapting to life as hunter-gatherers in the African savannah tens of thousands of years ago. Our bodies and minds are extremely flexible, so over the millennia we managed to readapt ourselves first to living as farmers in villages, and then to living as workers and service-providers in big cities. But it seems that the current pace of technological changes, and the resulting stress, are pushing Homo sapiens to its limits. We are no longer able to adapt fast enough. Hence the next big revolution of history is likely to be the revolution of humanity itself. When we think about the future we generally think about a world in which people who are identical to us in every important way enjoy better technology: laser guns, intelligent robots, and spaceships that travel at the speed of light. Yet the truly revolutionary potential of future technologies is to change Homo sapiens, including our bodies and our minds, and not merely our vehicles and weapons. The most amazing thing about the future won't be the spaceships, but the beings flying them.

Radical changes in human physical and cognitive abilities will probably begin to happen in the next few decades. Within a century or two, Homo sapiens will disappear, and will be replaced by completely different kinds of beings. Beings more different from us than we are different from Neanderthals.

Excerpt from the interview with Yuval Harari in "Abstrakt No 14" *Forever – On The Art Of Longevity*, Publisher: NZZ Verlag, 2015, Editor: W.I.R.E.

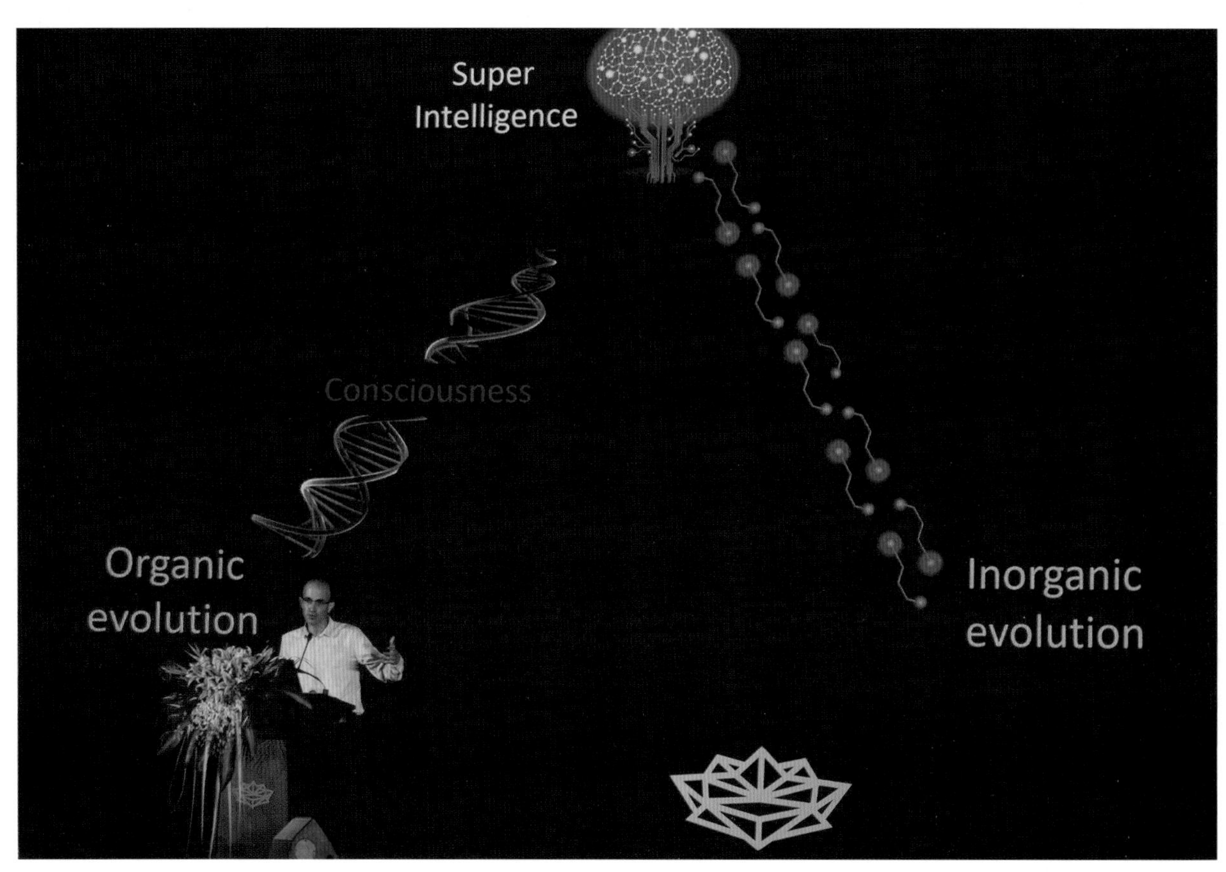

Yuval Noah Harari lectures on artificial intelligence in Hangzhou, Zhejiang Province of China.

YUVAL NOAH HARARI
is a senior lecturer in history at the Hebrew University of Jerusalem. He conducts research into military history and develops models of world history and macro-historical processes. In his best-seller on human history, "Sapiens: A Brief History of Humankind", he surveys the evolution of Homo sapiens from early times to the present.

BELGA MAG/AFP via Getty Images

SKILLS AND PERSONALISATION

LABOUR OF LOVE

JACQUELINE SEALY

Bespoke tailoring is more than taking people's measurements. It is understanding them as a whole, their imperfections, wishes, needs to show them in their best light. This is something machines will not be able to do – at least for now, argues Jacqueline Sealy. The lecturer in bespoke tailoring at London College of Fashion talks about the increasing demand for bespoke in times of automation and how it embraces new technologies to become more affordable and sustainable.

YOU ARE TEACHING BESPOKE TAILORING AT LONDON SCHOOL OF FASHION. WHY?

For me, bespoke tailoring is a labour of love. The many hours we invest in making a garment with our own hands, the appreciation of the handmade fabric we transform and the respect we have for the personalities and bodies of the people for whom we are making the clothes.

TODAY, WE CAN BUY MASS-MADE-TO-MEASURE SUITS ONLINE – FOR MUCH LESS MONEY. WHAT ARE THE CONSEQUENCES FOR THE FUTURE OF YOUR WORK?

I do not believe that automated production is a real challenge to bespoke tailoring. Even mass-made-to-measure, with which we are frequently compared, is no real risk. Actually, it is two pairs of shoes.

"If we had to advertise for bespoke tailoring in the future: Made for humans by humans."

JACQUELINE SEALY

WHAT IS THE DIFFERENCE?

In made-to-measure, a company simply uses a base pattern and adjusts it to your measurements. In bespoke, you get measured personally and then they make a pattern for you. Also, in this process, we not only take into consideration people's measurements, but also how they move, how they sit, if they have an old sports injury or a slightly hunched back, one leg longer than the other or one shoulder higher than the other. A bespoke tailor sees these "imperfections" immediately and makes people look good with them. That is one of the most important things we teach our students: To develop an experienced eye for the human body and the special needs of a client. Moreover, a person buying a bespoke suit has three to four fittings, meaning they come back, try their half-finished garment, and we get back to work. In mass-made-to-measure, there is no fitting at all. And machines don't understand imperfection.

WHAT DO YOU THINK OF ALGORITHMS THAT HELP US SHOP ONLINE BY SHOWING US VIRTUALLY WHETHER A GARMENT WILL FIT US?

So far, technology has not managed to advise us properly in buying clothes. If I buy online, I always buy several sizes, so that one of them hopefully fits. Also, not all people like their shirt fitted, some like it loose or oversized. Of course, in the future, programmes will get better, the body size will be measured more accurately, preferences remembered. Nevertheless, we cannot underestimate the fact that we are buying cloth, something we put on our bodies. And this is best bought with all our senses. When people go to a store, they like to feel the garment, hold it against the skin, see how it looks when you stand, when you sit. With increasing contact allergies, people want to see the reaction of their bodies before they buy. Also in terms of colours: So far there is no way of seeing colours realistically online.

IF PROGRAMS DO GET BETTER AND ALGORITHMS DESIGN CLOTHES BASED ON OUR MEASUREMENTS, HOW WILL THE FUTURE OF CLOTHING LOOK?

Standardised. If we are all having clothes made on our measurements, we are heading towards a more uniform look. We do want something different by personalising a garment to our body. But if all is fitted, none is personal and we will look more the same than ever. This is a chance for bespoke tailoring. In reaction to increasing homogenisation created by the mass market – even if made-to-measure – people will want to stand out as individuals. And bespoke offers exactly this: It is something made for individuals in the sense that it reflects their personalities, wishes, dreams. In recent years, bespoke

An experienced eye for the human body is still the most important skill for a bespoke tailor today: Sean Connery being fitted by the tailor Anthony Sinclair, 1963.

has become popular to a wider clientele, not only in clothing, but also in furniture, cars and jewellery. To have a car in your favourite colour, with your favourite fabric and furnished with your favourite wood is what people consider luxury – as difference in times of standardisation can only be achieved through true individualisation.

"Machines don't understand imperfection."

JACQUELINE SEALY

WILL BESPOKE TAILORING ALSO EMBRACE SMART CLOTHING?

It seems like the perfect match, as it is individualisation at its highest: Looks and function become personalised. This can range from traditional attributes – one of my students developed a functionalised front pocket, which sends out an alarm if the wallet gets stolen – to performance devices for athletes, like heart beat control. But as different as people are, as various are their needs and wishes, some will love their functionalised suits, others will deliberately decide against them.

DO YOU SEE ANY CHANGE IN THE CLIENTELE FOR BESPOKE CLOTHING?

We live in a world in which people want things very quickly. Bespoke takes time. Nevertheless, people are starting to appreciate this lengthy process again. They like the idea of having something individualised for them. The reason for this could, on the one hand, be found on an increasing wish for quality – in times of fast fashion. On the other hand, some people have more money than they used to. Especially the age group of 25 plus, if they have families later and are educated better, can afford to invest more in their look. The decision for bespoke is a decision to invest more. And that depends on how deep your pockets are. Nevertheless, individualisation can also be achieved on a smaller scale by taking advantage of new technologies. Our students use 3D printing to create personalised buttons, for example, resembling the future owner's wife. If you add such a button to a made-to-measure suit, you get a personalised garment at a much lower price. Also, the design process is increasingly done with virtual reality programs. In this way, customers can see exactly how their garment will look – whereas without such a program, several prototypes must be made to get the perfect solution. This means in the future we will use less material, which means less money and, of course, less waste!

TALKING OF SUSTAINABILITY: IS BESPOKE A SOLUTION FOR A MORE SUSTAINABLE CONSUMER BEHAVIOUR AS WE VALUE PERSONALISED GARMENTS MORE?

Absolutely. Bespoke garments are usually kept for a very long time and in many cases are passed down to the next generation as personal heritage. So far, however, it has been mainly men who buy bespoke – and who keep their clothes. They make adjustments, go and refit their suit, if necessary. We women, generally, invest more in the variety than the quality. Fast fashion was invented for women! Nevertheless, many women also appreciate the idea of having something made personally for them. In fact, the teaching of bespoke tailoring was predominantly for male clothing; now it is fifty-fifty. This trend could certainly lead to more sustainable consumer behaviour.

BESPOKE TAILORING HAS BEEN VERY TRADITIONAL IN TERMS OF GENDER BINARY. HOW IS THIS GOING TO CHANGE IN THE CONTEXT OF AN INCREASING TREND TOWARDS GENDER NEUTRAL CLOTHING?

There will be a true shift in the way gender is displayed in clothing. Bespoke tailoring has indeed been rather traditional in terms of gender. Today we have more and more students designing gender-neutral garments. This does not only break with traditional gender representation in clothing but also with the focus on the shape of the body. The future tailors are using unisex patterns, some of which are rather oversized, that can be worn by male and female customers. The personalisation then happens at a different level – beyond the confines of the body type – for example, through special colours, materials and functions – or through the whole shape of the piece of clothing being unique.

WHAT IS THE VALUE OF HUMAN LABOUR IN A PIECE OF CLOTH?

If we know who made a garment, especially if it was personally made for us, it gains more sentimental value. We feel connected with it and with the people who invested their labour in it. When you go for a fitting, you enter a relationship with the tailors and they with us – with our personalities, preferences, stories. It is this personal touch, which makes people feel valued. A feeling that can, to some degree, be compared to going to a hairdresser – only more so. If we put this in a context of increasing automation and artificial intelligence, it all comes down to feeling human, not feeling like a robot. If we had to advertise for bespoke tailoring in the future, the slogan might be: Made for humans by humans!

WHAT SKILLS WILL YOU TEACH YOUR STUDENTS IN THE FUTURE – IN COMPARISON TO NOW?

They will still need to understand the basic principles of cutting, shaping and fitting: how to handstitch, how to insert a sleeve, how a jacket needs to hang on the body when it's fitted, how to look at clients and analyse how they move. These old skills of understanding the fabric, how to treat it and how it relates to the human body won't change much. However, in the future there will also be usage of artificial intelligence: machines that mimic handcraft, for example. The question is, how precise they will become and how much of that "personal touch" is lost on the way. Some of our students learn how to develop a piece of garment virtually. The way they do it is mind-blowing. Nevertheless: They have to know the skills of bespoke to make bespoke digitally. But no matter how much is going to change in our teachings: We need to keep up with the times, to understand new and different customer's needs. Some people might enjoy coming in three or four times for fitting, others will want to take advantage of new technology and do this virtually.

"These old skills of understanding the fabric, how to treat it and how it relates to the human body won't change much."

JACQUELINE SEALY

SO NO RADICAL CHANGE IN THE FUTURE OF CLOTHING IN SIGHT?

I think we are going round in circles, as fashion and trends often do. If radical change happens, there will be a time when other things happen that bring it back to basics. Take fast fashion, for example: People will realise they are being cheated, that these garments are not made to last and can ultimately cost us more money than high-quality clothing. Eventually we will learn that less is more and put more emphasis on quality than quantity – until the next trend occurs.

JACQUELINE SEALY

is a former course leader for the BA(hons) Bespoke Tailoring course at London College of Fashion, University of the Arts London. She has been at the university since 1994 and has a long history in course leadership roles, including Further Education Pattern and Garment Technology. This course introduced students to the concept of how patterns and garments are developed using modern technology. Sealy has over 30 years of pattern cutting, 3D realisation and product development skills within both men's and women's wear. Jacqueline's teaching philosophy is to creatively challenge and be challenged by students to give them a firm foundation to pursue a career in the fashion industry of the future.

LUXURY AND BUSINESS

OF LUXURY AND ETERNITY

JEAN-CLAUDE BIVER

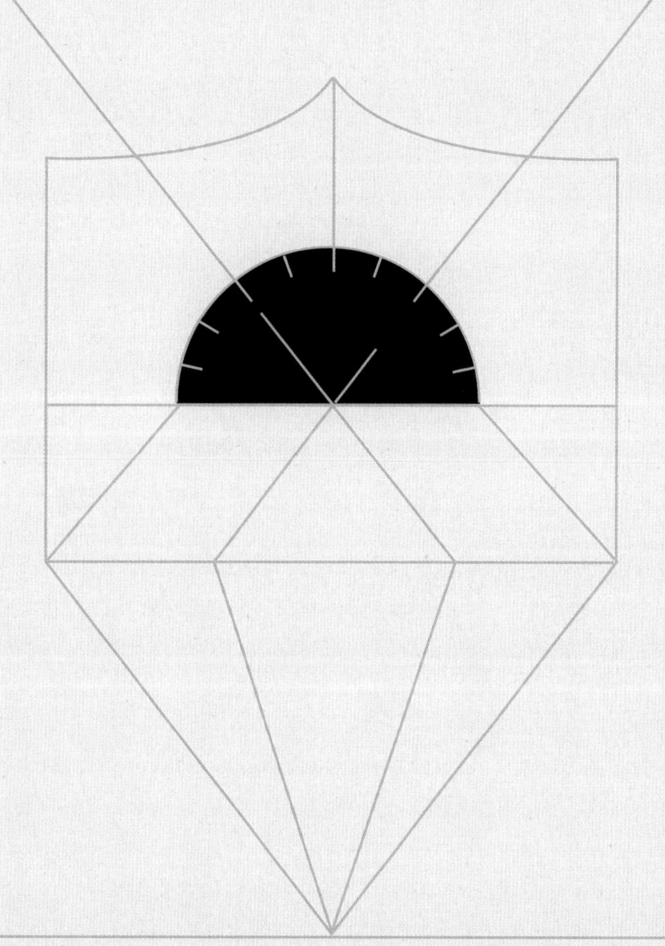

Luxury will be available at various levels in the future and an increasing number of people will be climbing up that ladder: from high-end industrial goods, over the semi-individualised like mass-made-to-measure, through to the truly personalised and unique. For companies to have a range in the top segment requires the courage to infuse tradition with future design and establish a culture of mistakes, says Jean-Claude Biver, the CEO of TAG Heuer®. And to leave their goods in the hands of humans – as only humans can bestow them with a soul.

HOW WILL LUXURY TOMORROW COMPARE TO TODAY?

To answer that we have to define what luxury is – a discussion that would take us more than an our, more likely a week. So the only thing I can offer you is a personal view of luxury. I believe that the ultimate luxury is the same for everyone, today and in the future. That is: To be alive and in good health and to love and be loved. And: to be aware of this. No money in the world can buy any of these things. Nor can we be happy without them – rich or not. A wealthy man can afford a better cancer therapy than the poor, but – on average – this only prolongs his life for a few months or years. He also has better chances to attract a beautiful woman, but to make her love him, that is a different story. The problem with this perception of luxury is: Nobody earns money with it.

NONETHELESS: THE TREND TOWARDS A HEALTHY LIFESTYLE, FROM YOGA TO VEGANISM, SHOWS THAT PEOPLE ARE SEARCHING FOR MORE THAN MATERIAL CONSUMER GOODS. AND THAT MONEY CAN BE EARNED WITH THE CORRESPONDING PRODUCTS.

I agree. However, we are talking of a small amount of people here. Also, buying yoga leggings does not automatically make you a satisfied person. There is no problem with buying consumer products if we don't confuse them with a happy life. What I do find problematic, however, is what is sold to people under the label of luxury. In the last thirty years there was a shift towards what I like to call marketing-luxury: mass produced products, often of poor quality, get sold as high-end goods. As a result of this development, real luxury – with reference to products – can go unrecognized. In many cases, the creators of real luxury – I call them artists – who focus purely on their skills and the quality of their goods, are overlooked in the midst of all the glossy ads inflating cheap industrial products. In my opinion, luxury has to be based on tradition, heritage, art, quality, soul and eternity.

THAT SOUNDS CHALLENGING. HOW DOES A PRODUCT GET A SOUL AND BECOME ETERNAL?

We cannot explain this rationally, as we cannot describe rationally the human soul. But we can feel it. It is spiritual – to put it vaguely. And products can and should be spiritual, too. Every item made by a human can reflect the maker's personality. The tailor gives a suit or a dress their soul, skill, and authenticity. A product made exclusively and 100% by a machine will never have the same emotional effect on us. Under these conditions, the number of brands in the luxury segment is reduced dramatically.

AND WHAT ABOUT ETERNITY?

A product with a soul is eternal: If it is the first watch our parents gave us, with the clockwork still ticking, or a bespoke suit that has been made for us and that will remind our grandchildren of our existence. The problem with many industrial products is that they are born programmed to become obsolete. Technical products are especially short lived, as technology always kills the antecedent generation. I remember watching television with my family in the 1960s. Suddenly, the football players were in colour! Black and white television got killed by colour TV. We are observing the same today with computers, cell phones, iPads – only now the killing happens at much shorter intervals. A connected watch will one day become outdated. If we compare it to the watches made by the famous clockmaker Abraham-Louis Breguet, who made watches for queens and kings throughout Europe in the 18th century – these technologies still work. And even if they did not: These watches reflect the spirit of their inventor, his craftsmanship and genius. They will survive us.

THAT MEANS: DIGITALISATION AND AUTOMATION WILL NEVER PLAY A MAJOR ROLE IN THE MAKING OF PROPER LUXURY?

It depends on how these "tools" are used. Tradition needs three things. First: people or companies that keep them alive. When nobody listens to Mozart, his music will die. Second: It needs an interface with the present. A mere repetition of the old keeps it in the past. A product needs to relate to the society and culture it is embedded in, if it is to retain its value. That means we need to bring in elements of today, for example by embracing new technologies to improve the tradition. If

Mozart crawled out of his grave and saw our modern instruments he would thank us, as they make his music sound better. It's the same with watchmaking. Today we work with much more precision than 200 years ago, for example, we replaced magnifying glasses with high tech microscopes. But using these instruments does not take away the soul of the watch; it only increases the quality.

AND THIRD?

Sometimes we need to break the tradition to give birth to a new one. This does not mean losing your roots, but it means enforcing the fusion between yesterday and today. To achieve this takes courage. You need to know your tradition and to anticipate the future – and bring the two together. At Hublot, for example, we are still making watches, all of them with our hands. But we broke our tradition a few years ago with the material we are using. Gold, from Tutankhamun until some years ago, has been soft and got scratched. An old Collier could be recognized by the its scratches. We at Hublot said: We want gold, 18 carat, but no more scratches! So we revolutionised the material and now the only diamonds can harm our gold. But we don't deal with diamonds every day, right?

AT THE OTHER END OF PRODUCTS FOR ETERNITY IS FAST FASHION, A TREND THAT HAS ALSO REACHED THE PREMIUM SEGMENT. HOW DO YOU JUDGE THIS DEVELOPMENT?

It depends on the quality of the product. If it remains at high level, pace is an advantage without harm. In the watch business, for example, 10 watches are exclusive. But one hundred watches

Whereas smart watches quickly become outdated, handmade, mechanical ones keep their value – not for their practicability, but as an artwork. Here we see one of the few tourbillons by Abraham-Louis Breguet (pocket watch no. 1176), made in the 18th century.

are also exclusive. So I can sell more and lose nothing – meaning technology here is a good investment. With reference to fast fashion, pace is essential – at the cost of quality, of course. But in this case, quality means a different thing. Consumers of such products do not buy their clothes to keep them, but to be trendy. The question that arises, though, is: How innovative can fashion be if it has to develop new styles at such small intervals? To create something truly new takes time.

HOW CAN WE ACHIEVE MORE INNOVATION OTHER THAN BY INVESTING MORE TIME?

By making mistakes. From childhood on we are told not to make mistakes. That means living in constant fear, the fear of doing something wrong. This is paralyzing in the sense that we tend to follow the paths we know. We cannot possibly find new solutions, products, ideas in this way. So we have to let go of that fear and become more open. Moreover, the mistakes themselves are a vital source for innovation. They do not only tell us how to do things better, when we get lucky, they also tell us how to do things in another, better way. I used to pay my employees for making mistakes to make them more courageous.

RECENT TECHNOLOGICAL ADVANCES HAVE ALLOWED THE SEMI-PERSONALISATION OF MASS PRODUCTS, SUCH AS MASS-MADE-TO-MEASURE CLOTHES: A TRUE BREAKTHROUGH?

In the last century, luxury was always personal in the sense that it was one of a kind. With the arrival of industrial luxury products this changed – which is not only a bad thing, I have to admit. It

"A product needs to relate to the society and culture it is embedded in."

JEAN-CLAUDE BIVER

was the attempt to make luxury more accessible. Before, only the richest people could afford it. In addition, this mass luxury has the positive side effect that there are more and more companies which want to distance themselves from it. Luxury exists at various levels, and will be even more so tomorrow. It comes in the shape of a pyramid: On the bottom we find expensive mass-produced products, at the top is the handmade and fully personalised and in the middle there will be the semi-personalised goods like mass-made-to-measure. They are not exclusive. But the possibility of part-individualisation allows an increasing number of people to climb to the next level in the luxury pyramid. That is a positive development.

YOU RATE THE HANDMADE AT THE TOP: WHAT ROLE DO YOU SEE FOR CRAFTSMANSHIP IN THE FUTURE?

I am fascinated with humans, their hands and what they can do with them. To me, as mentioned before, a product made by someone's hands is true and forever. So I cannot imagine a future in which craftsmanship plays no role. I make cheese every year in the Swiss Alps. Cheese making is based on a tradition that dates back hundreds of years ago; the recipe I follow is from 1150. The process of making cheese in a traditional way connects us to the people who lived before us. And it connects us to the nature and the animals around us. A variety of components are of importance: where and at which height the grass grows, what sort it is, how the farmer treats and feeds the animals, how clean they are. If we put it that way, craftsmanship can teach us how to respect each other and our environment and together create something truly valuable.

WATCHES AND CLOTHES SHARE THE SAME PROPERTIES: THEY ARE WORN ON OUR BODIES, BASED ON OLD CRAFTSMANSHIP, USED AS STATUS SYMBOLS. HOW DOES THE FUTURE OF CLOTHING LOOK LIKE IN YOUR EYES AS A "WATCH"-MAN?

I believe most innovation and renewal in the field of clothing will be around new material. Material is the base of any garment and I have been astonished how little evolution it has undergone in the last decades. All the focus was on fashion, too little on the fabric. My Cortex sports garments protect me from rain, yes, but I get soaked nevertheless – from my own sweat. I'd rather be wet from rain! Cashmere is also a good example for lack of innovation. I love cashmere. But why can I not wear it in the rain? Because that is how it is, I am told. That is no answer to me. Today, in the context of increasing digitalisation and the search for new material to interlink clothing with our technical devices change is on the horizon. Finally!

THERE ARE RUMOURS THAT THE SMART PHONE WILL BE REPLACED BY CLOTHES. WHAT DO YOU THINK?

I believe that the smart phone will die. I am not sure it will be replaced by clothes only, though. There will be a competition between watches and clothes. Clothing could provide us with everything, health devices, communication, heating and cooling. However, the watch has various advantages over clothing: you can wear it for a whole year without washing, you can sleep in it without changing and you only need one. With clothes people want more variety and they need to clean them regularly. When it comes to cooling and heating or any other form of protecting the body, the clothes will obviously win.

HOW CAN TRADITIONAL COMPANIES IN THE FIELD OF CLOTHING AND ACCESSORIES PREPARE FOR THE FUTURE?

We need to stay true to our roots but also open our eyes for change. And, most importantly, listen to the young. Everybody is saying it but nobody does it. Most long-established companies believe they know their business. But when you believe you know something you are already left behind. How long did it take the Catholic Church before they decided not to hold the service in Latin? The same resistance prevails in companies. How many millenials sit on the board of directors? In most cases none. That is a fatal mistake. We don't give the young their say, even though our future depends on them.

IF YOU HAD A WISH: WHAT FUTURE GARMENT WOULD YOU LIKE TO POSSESS?

Something that cools and warms me so that I don't have to wear three layers to move around. That would be pure comfort – luxury! And it should look decent, too. Ideally a cashmere that I'd wear on a rainy walk with my dog.

JEAN-CLAUDE BIVER

is a Luxembourgish watchmaker and businessman currently serving as the CEO of TAG Heuer. In January 2014, he became president of Louis Vuitton's watchmaking division. Previously he has been CEO of Hublot, where he established the philosophy of the "fusion of tradition and future". Previously he was responsible for the brand rejuvenation at OMEGA, which he promoted with product placements in James Bond movies and through celebrities like Cindy Crawford and Pierce Brosnan. Biver is famous for unusual business methods, like paying people for making mistakes. Every year, Biver produces approximately five tonnes of cheese at his farm in the Swiss Alps.

LUXURY AND CRAFTSMANSHIP

TOWARDS LONGEVITY AND PERFORMANCE

GREGOR THISSEN

Garments need to work harder in the future. They have to be comfortable, enhance our life and look good, says Gregor Thissen, Executive Chairman of the cloth merchant and expert tailor Scabal. And they need to last longer, as ecologically aware customers are getting tired of fast fashion. New man-made materials and the rediscovery of the benefits of various natural fibres will play a vital role in fusing performance, aesthetics and sustainability. For the luxury segment, the goal for the future is to embrace new technologies while staying true to established quality standards.

IN YOUR OPINION, WHAT FACTORS ARE MAINLY SHAPING THE FUTURE OF CLOTHING AND CLOTH?

The fact that people have a much faster pace of life, which makes different demands on their clothing requirements. Time-short lifestyles mean that clothes need to work harder and suit more occasions – from gym, to work, a quick run to the shopping centre and off to the inauguration of a new museum. This has dramatically changed what kinds of fabrics are being developed. Previously, the focus for a luxury fabric producer was on creating ever more fine wools or finding ways of weaving delicate materials like vicuna and cashmere; now finding the best performance, for example with natural stretch or crease-resistant technologies, plays an equally important role. Casualisation of clothing has also had an impact on what people are wearing and looking for in their garments.

Customers want clothes that are increasingly comfortable to wear. This is challenging suppliers of formal clothes to widen their collections, introduce and explore elements of sportswear to create outfits which still have a sartorial basis but with a less formal attitude.

BESIDES BECOMING LESS FORMAL, WHAT CHARACTERISES THE CLOTHES OF THE FUTURE, IN LUXURY AND BEYOND?

Customisation has put the individual consumer at the centre of considerations for producers and brands alike, hence asking for ever more flexibility and depth of choice. As a result, formal dress codes will soften even further. In the future there will be a much wider array of styles and designers and brands will no longer be the only trend-setters. But to a certain extent, the needs of all customers – regardless of where they sit in the marketplace – will be similar. Besides the desire for more comfort and individuality, people will want clothes that last longer. We can see a certain tiredness of fast fashion in the market. A stronger sense of responsibility for the future of our planet has a lot of luxury and non-luxury customers thinking about the aberration of throwing away a t-shirt after one season because it does not hold its shape.

Technical functionality will also play a vital role in the future of clothing. The focus will be on garments that can enhance your life, like those made from medical monitoring fabrics, or which make life easier, such as cell phone-free communication. The challenge will be to find ways beyond built-in devices, such as weaving the sensors directly into the fabric – a method that is currently being developed by various start-ups.

But we should also consider the possibility that in a certain niche, classical sartorial clothing will make a return. Within this world of technology, globalisation and digital, people might just want to be able to rely on some good old classics, made according to age-old standards and methods. Just like the watchmaker or the bespoke shoemaker, the recurrence of the traditional master tailor might be more than just a dream.

WILL SMART CLOTHING ALSO EMBRACE THE LUXURY SEGMENT?

Luxury is driven by beauty and, until technology is sleek enough to fit within the luxury aesthetic, it will remain as an accompaniment. However, once the size of the battery or power source can be reduced, luxury will certainly embrace smart clothing – and lead the way. Luxury brands have the customers who want and can afford to be at the forefront of all new developments and it makes sense for the clothes they wear to be as advanced as the rest of their life. We are currently working on a research project to create an intelligent fabric which could conduct a charge. It is an experiment for us and, like many visionary projects, it is difficult to predict the outcome, but it could lead to all sorts of practical applications like conducting light or making the cloth a direct medium for communications or data transfer.

IN RECENT YEARS WE HAVE WITNESSED THE DEVELOPMENT OF NEW MATERIALS SUCH AS SPIDER SILK AND LAB-GROWN LEATHER. HOW MUCH POTENTIAL IS THERE FOR INNOVATION IN THIS FIELD?

“When you are dealing with luxury fabrics, touch and feel are discriminating factors.”

GREGOR THISSEN

Increases in world population and wealth will create a much higher demand for both man-made and natural raw materials. With many natural products we will probably reach the physical limits of availability. Already today we are witnessing over-farming for cotton, cashmere and other noble fibres. The development of new man-made alternatives that are inspired by, or even mimic, the extraordinary complexity of nature's inventions, could provide a welcome alternative. Hybrid forms like spider silk could combine the best of both worlds, by preserving precious natural resources and yet fulfilling increasing demand for products with natural attributes. There are many lessons to be learned from nature, be it from the highly resistant but yet flexible fibrous structure of the bamboo tree or the moisture-sensitive transformation mechanisms of a pine cone, which opens when dried and closes when wet. Numerous research projects are under way that will help the industry to satisfy the growing demand and become more sustainable at the same time. However, we believe that natural materials will still have a place and hopefully even more so in the future.

MUCH OF THE DIALOGUE ABOUT THE FUTURE OF CLOTHING IS CENTRED ON AUTOMATION. SEWING ROBOTS ARE GETTING BETTER, MASS-MADE-TO-MEASURE ARE MAKING CUSTOMISED SUITS AFFORDABLE. HOW DO YOU DEAL WITH THIS CHALLENGE?

We don't see mass automation as a challenge, but more of another way of segmenting the marketplace between garments made in vast numbers and garments made with individual customers in mind. The real change is found in the general evolution of the customer's attitude to individualisation. Even in the mass-market segment, customers are looking for customisation. Sewing robots and further automation will help to fulfil this desire at their chosen price point. Luxury customers will also value individuality – for them it is almost a given – and they will want their bag, suit or shoes to be customised. Compared to the mass market, however, they will equally expect superior quality and exclusivity of raw materials and production techniques. This will automatically lead them to more crafted products made with finer fabrics and personalised down to the final detail. Once you understand this as a brand or producer, you will cater to these needs accordingly.

WHICH HUMAN FABRIC-MAKING SKILLS ARE GOING TO LAST IN THE NEXT DECADES?

Human skills will not only last, they will be regarded more highly in times of automation – as a potent way to differentiate from the mass market. In recent years, technology has helped to make certain tasks more efficient but, especially in the luxury segment, they are rather supporting the human skills of the craftsmen and women rather than replacing them. When you are dealing with luxury fabrics, touch and feel are discriminating factors. They need to be manually assessed throughout the whole manufacturing process. In fact, looms have become so fast that when we are creating some of our most luxurious fabrics we actually slow them down so that the delicate yarns are not put under stress as they are woven. This results in a fabric without any flaws. From weaving through mending and finishing to the final control, at every stage we need a human eye and touch to intervene – to guarantee that the final consumer will be satisfied with our product.

SO HUMANS WILL REMAIN ESSENTIAL IN THE LUXURY CLOTHING MARKET OF TOMORROW?

In the luxury market the human element remains vital from the point of sale through production. Our in-store teams guide the customers through the stages of choosing a personalised garment – starting with the choice of fabrics, customers don't only make their choices through the colour or design but through touch and feel as well. When we take their measurements it takes a trained eye to collate all the precise measures needed to ensure that the garment fits and feels as personal as possible. In production, the expert teams make patterns for individual customers; the fabric cutters have to understand the way the cloth hangs and, in tailoring, hand sewing conveys a very different look and feel to a machine-sewn garment.

During my early years of training, one of my teachers told me that, despite the advanced technology in dying techniques, at the end it was still down to the experience of the head-dyer to ensure perfect consistency of colour, something that needs to be judged with the eye in the correct light. This is still true today. Of course, technology will progress and it will and should be used wherever it can help to perfect the end-product or facilitate the life of the customer – without taking away the "human touch" of a luxury product.

"Clothing needs to appeal to emotions."

GREGOR THISSEN

WHAT ROLE DOES DIGITALISATION PLAY IN YOUR BUSINESS NOW AND HOW DO YOU EXPECT IT TO CHANGE IN THE FUTURE?

Digitalisation has definitely helped promote tailoring to a wider audience. The exposure of the famous Pitti Peacocks – fashion-conscious individuals parading around the major menswear Trade Fair "Pitti Uomo" – for example, has increased dramatically thanks to social media. Combined with the rise in popularity of tailoring blogs and online influencers, this has helped bring a younger focus to formal dressing, creating a modern form of Dandyism and male expression of elegance.

From a business point of view, we rely on digital tools to enhance our service levels. We have online ordering tools for our partners, automated reporting to help us manage our inventory levels and iPads in all our stores so our sales teams can bring our fabrics to life for customers through photography and films. However, selling luxury made-to-measure suits online seems inappropriate even today. Certain efforts have been made, but at this stage the process and the results are not up to scratch. Should we get to the point where body scanners are sophisticated enough to take the precise measurements needed for tailoring we will certainly use them. However, I cannot see them completely replacing the eye of a tailor or the expert advice of a seasoned clothing adviser nor the feel of hand selecting the different materials needed to make a suit.

TALKING TO YOU AS A DESIGNER OF CLOTH AND CLOTHING: HOW WILL ARTIFICIAL INTELLIGENCE CHANGE THE PROCESS OF DESIGNING CLOTHES AND HOW CREATIVE WILL THE OUTCOME BE?

Clothing needs to appeal to emotions – it's not all about functionality and a computer will probably never be able to truly understand emotions. However, if AI was combined with human designers it might enhance their work or make it easier and quicker to turn their initial ideas into outcomes, which they could then refine Also, after so many years of fashion evolution, it is hard to see where a revolution would come from. Fashion is continuing to reinvent what has already been invented. The input of a machine might change this. Even though at the moment algorithms are programmed to merely reproduce what they are taught, in the future they might surprise us with new suggestions – maybe by unusually combining ideas of other fields with clothing.

WITH THE ONGOING DIY TREND IN MIND: WHAT ROLE DOES THE CONSUMER PLAY IN THE FUTURE OF DESIGN?

The luxury market is already focused on addressing customers on an almost one to one basis whether through entirely bespoke products or through personalisation and customisation opportunities. It makes sense that the mass market customer will also start seeking these options and that they are offered a more active role in the design process – whether this leads to customers creating their own designs with online design apps to print with their 3D printer or just giving opinions via social media channels on brands' potential collections. There is no doubt that the advance of technology is involving the customer more and more in the design and production of their purchase, but let us not forget that being a good designer needs a lot of talent, extensive training and very hard work. Not necessarily something that just anybody can replicate.

WHAT IS YOUR VISION OF THE FUTURE OF CLOTHING?

In 1971 when we asked Salvador Dalí to imagine the future of menswear he looked to the past to predict the future. For the most part, what he predicted reflected evolutions rather than revolutions. As we look forward again today in the context of so much new technology and environmental changes we feel in a less confident place to assume that what has come before will dictate what will be in the future. We believe that there will always be a place for luxury, however, customers will become more demanding of the performance and functionality of their clothes. The challenge for brands like us will be to embrace the technological advances whilst keeping the essence of what makes a garment special: the combination of the finest materials, expertise and craftsmanship in production and a beautiful finished presentation. And thankfully sustainability in the larger sense is now firmly established in people's minds and we can therefore be quite confident that the textile industry at large – cloth and clothing – will be a positive contributor to a cleaner world. Personalisation in its various shapes or forms will also play a major role and help people to keep or achieve a singular identity in a world that could elsewhere drift into uber-standardisation.

GREGOR THISSEN

Born in Germany, Gregor moved with his parents to Brussels in 1971 when his father, a second-generation fabric merchant, became a partner at Scabal. After studying Law in Germany and Business at a US University, Gregor spent a few years working in the corporate fields of insurance and banking, but in 1991 he returned to Brussels to join his father at Scabal. In 2006, Gregor took over as CEO, a position he continued until 2013, when he transitioned to his current role of Executive Chairman. An active member of YPO-WPO, an international peer network for entrepreneurs and company leaders, he has served in various functions on the board of the organisation. Next to his professional life, he spends as much time as possible with his family – his wife and four children – and when time allows he enjoys golf, tennis and soccer, being a founder member of the Scabal five-a-side team.

EXPERT THESES

Conclusion of the main opinions and insights

- 1 -
THERE WILL BE FUNDAMENTAL CHANGE IN THE FUNCTION OF CLOTHING AND THE FOCUS OF INNOVATION

Even though the developments ahead of us are not as disruptive as the industrialisation in the 19th century, clothing will undergo substantial change. On the one hand, the function is shifting. For the first time in the history of clothing, the two roles of garments, protection and status, are expanded by a third: the interaction of clothing with the wearer and their environment. On the other hand, the main goal of technological innovation – to increase efficiency – is joined by the new goals of sustainability, medicalisation and individuality.

- 2 -
THE VALUE OF HANDMADE CLOTHES WILL INCREASE AS A RESULT OF AUTOMATION AND MASS-MADE-TO-MEASURE

With the proceeding automation of the production of clothing and in response to two decades of cheap fashion, the handmade will become more precious. As customisation reaches the mass market with the help of virtualisation and automation, the luxury segment will distinguish itself with a new focus on handmade clothes, promising true individuality and personalisation beyond the mere measuring of the body. The demand for bespoke tailoring, in particular, will rise, also amongst a young clientele.

- 3 -
CONSUMER BEHAVIOUR WILL SHIFT TOWARDS BETTER QUALITY AND LONGEVITY

The number of people refusing to buy poor quality clothing will grow steadily and will eventually lead to an effective weakening of the market for fast fashion. As customers are becoming better informed they will recognise false markets and bad deals. Simultaneously, the demand for durable garments with a longer life span will shape the supply of mass markets. However, to bring good clothing to the high street, price barriers will have to be tackled; quality needs to become affordable.

- 4 -
THE QUEST FOR SUSTAINABILITY IN CLOTHING WILL BE SUCCESSFUL DUE TO MORE REGULATION, STRONGER ECOLOGICAL AWARENESS AND THE PROGRESS IN MATERIAL SCIENCE

A critical mass of consumers will be reached and the pressure on suppliers will be increased due to more regulation, higher transparency in the digital age and the customers' wish to identify with their brands. Important enablers are scientific and technological progress, the various new innovative materials and the digital sample-making in particular. The risks to the quest for sustainability will be greenwashing and the possible persistence or reappearance of a market for fast fashion.

- 5 -
VIRTUALISATION AND AUTOMATION WILL HAVE A DISRUPTIVE EFFECT ON THE PRODUCTION OF COMMODITY CLOTHING BY MAKING IT LESS DEPENDENT ON HUMAN LABOUR

The technological progress in the production of clothing will be comparable to the invention of the power loom in the 19th century. As most tasks in the production of clothing will be automated and sewing machines will improve their performance, we will witness a fundamental shift away from today's high dependency on human labour. However, the human role in making and designing clothes will remain important. In the luxury segment, machines will have to content themselves with the jobs of assistants; the human eye and hand will remain superior in judging the quality and cuts of materials and process fine textiles.

- 6 -
FUNCTIONALISATION WILL PLAY A PREVAILING ROLE IN THE FUTURE OF CLOTHING BUT WILL HAVE TO ADDRESS TECHNOLOGICAL AND CULTURAL BARRIERS TO REACH THE MASS MARKET

The benefits of merging clothing with the health sector and communication will become obvious in context of an aging population, the ongoing digitalisation and the creation of smart environments. However, despite the progress in the miniaturisation of sensors, the goal of making circuits truly invisible will take time. If these technological challenges are not tackled and prices remain high, functional clothing will position itself in specific fields of the health sector and the luxury segment. Also, the fear of too much dependency on technology might frustrate the entry of smart clothing into the mass market.

- 7 -
THE HUMAN BODY AND BRAIN WILL UNDERGO A REVOLUTION; THE WEARERS OF TOMORROW'S CLOTHES WILL BE A DIFFERENT SPECIES

The next fundamental change in the history of humanity will concern humanity itself. Whereas today we still have the same body and mind as our ancestors in the Roman Empire, in the coming decades, for the first time in history, our bodies and minds will be transformed by genetic engineering, nanotechnology and brain–computer interfaces. The result will be a new human species and thus a new species to be dressed.

- 8 -
THE HUMAN AND ITS SENSES WILL BE REDISCOVERED

The value of the human senses will grow in the digital age and lead to a bigger awareness of the importance of the material of clothes and the way they feel on the skin. Whereas virtual fitting rooms will become standard for online shopping, a growing number of customers will want to touch the fabric before purchasing it. In general, there will be a desire to be treated as humans by humans as the human identity will be strengthened in the machine age.

"The ages that looked the most avidly to their future, were those that recorded the passing of time with the most splendid fashion."

SALVADOR DALÍ

LADY GODIVA FULLY CLOTHED MAY NOW JOIN
THE PILGRIMAGE TO SANTIAGO DE COMPOSTELLA

A NETWORK OF SOFT TOGGLES AND CRAVATES FOR THE FINANCIAL SUCCESS OF THE NEXT RICHELIEU

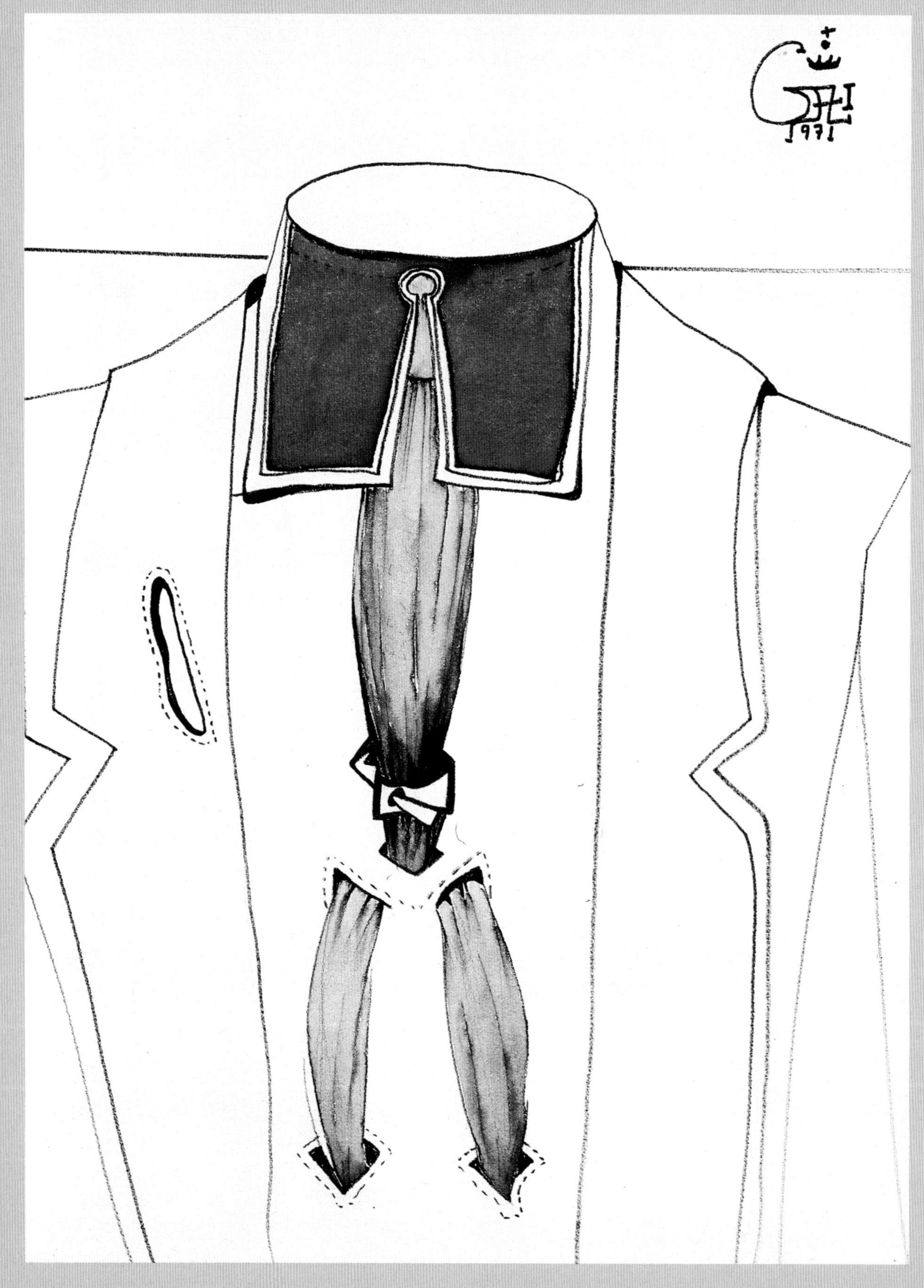

"Here clothes make the man; there man makes the clothes."

SALVADOR DALÍ

III

FROM PROTECTION TO INTERACTION

SCENARIOS FOR THE 22ND CENTURY

The future is not set in stone. First, it does not exist – yet. And second, we are actively adding to its formation. To shape the world of tomorrow, we have to create spaces of opportunity. For this purpose, we have to imagine where the current changes, if they were to be continued, might lead us. At the heart of this discussion is not the practicability of the new technologies and trends, but their desirability. The question is how we *want* the future to look, rather than how it *will* look. The following seven scenarios and illustrations of possible futures help to lay the foundation for an active and critical engagement with the clothing of tomorrow.

N°1

LONGEVITY OVER FASHION

A SUIT FOR A LIFETIME

With increasing awareness of the ecological effects of the fashion business and the growing refusal to accept poor quality, clothing will move away from fast fashion to slow and no fashion. There will be a growing demand and market for high quality fabric and garments that are independent of changing style and seasons. The fusion of crafted clothes and innovative tailoring with integrated circuits and new materials such as artificial spider silk or lotus fibres will take a leading role in this development: Suits that can be worn for indoor and outdoor activities, pants which grow or shrink according to the way our body changes, water-repellent and super strong fabrics that stay clean and cannot fall apart. As a result, garments will be like best buddies that accompany us in any life situation and over our increasingly long life. Whereas everything else changes, including environments and people, clothes will remain and support us until the very end. True sustainability will depend not only on how ecologically a garment is produced, but also on how long we are able to keep and wear it.

N°2

CUSTOMERS AS DESIGNERS

TOWARDS AUTARKY

Over recent decades we have witnessed an ongoing DIY-trend in clothing and beyond. The wish to have something individualised and to make a product with one's own hands will become even more important in the context of an increasingly digitised environment. Unlike in the past, however, new technologies will complement sewing and stitching and allow people with minimal manual skills or time to create their own garments. 3D printers and intelligent design tools, which take our measurements and analyse our preference and come up with design suggestions, will change the rules and roles of the fashion business. Customers will no longer only be recipients but also designers and producers. To draw your shirt online, based on the recommendations of AI, and print it directly with your home 3D printer will soon be a reality. As a result, the dependency on external companies is fading, the foundations laid for a self-sustaining supply of clothing.

N°3

ENHANCED PROTECTION

CLOTHES AS ALARM SYSTEMS

The primary function of clothing has always been to protect the wearer from heat, cold, water and wind by putting a layer between the body and the external environment. In the future, clothes will do much more than this: They will be our additional senses that warn us of risks our own senses fail to recognize. On the one hand, garments will collect and analyse our body's reactions, like heart beats or sweat, regulate our body temperature through cooling down or warming up the fabric, and inform us when we're over strained or stressed. On the other hand, they will pick up new and old man-made environmental risks, such as smog or a new virus and advise us to wear a mask, keep social distance or seek protection. Sewn-in sensors will make a smart garment out of any piece of clothing, from casual sport dress to bespoke suit. Like exoskeletons made of fabric, clothes will shield us from harm – from the inside and the outside. As a side effect, human enhancement will shift away from cyborgisation to smart clothing: not body implants but garments are leading the way to the future.

N°4

DRESSING THE NEXT GENERATION

SUITS FOR ROBOTS

Not only will the styles, materials and functions of clothes change, but also their future wearers. With the increasing pervasiveness of robots in our everyday lives, the intelligent machines surrounding us will be dressed in order to appear more humane and lovable. Robots used in healthcare or households, for example, will need special health uniforms or aprons in order to be accepted by the patients or the families. Currently, one of the most successful robots in healthcare comes in the shape of a furry seal, cute to the eye and soft to the touch. With the enhancement of robots, a next generation of robots with distinct personalities and distinct styles will evolve, from street wear to the business suit for machines. The effect will be an increasing demand for clothes and the development of new niches.

N°5

CRAFTSMANSHIP AS LUXURY

CLOTHING BEYOND AUTOMATION

As a result of the increasing digitalisation of our environment and the growing automation of work, tangibles like well-made textiles will become more important. Special skills, like weaving and knitting, will be seen as "old arts" and gain in appreciation. Moreover, in times of mass-made-to-measure, luxury in the clothing sector will have to be more than a well-fitted suit. Luxury, in the sense of exclusiveness and as a symbol of social status, will be based on high quality material, true personalisation beyond the customer's measurements and on the quality of work that was invested in the garment. Differentiation in times of automation will be achieved through hand-crafted goods; the human labour is what makes a suit or a dress unique. Innovative tailoring techniques, making use of the latest technology, such as smart fibres, will complement traditional fabrics to make clothes even more individualised and will pave the way for a new modernised era of craftsmanship.

N°6

LOCAL FAST FASHION

THE END OF "MADE IN TAIWAN"

The industrial revolution radically changed the production of clothes and made garments affordable for the less wealthy. Today, we are on the brink of the next fundamental change in the history of clothing. Automated production with sewing robots will reduce the cost of manufacturing dramatically as much less human resources will be needed. Moreover, modern computer-aided design programs will not only make mass-production cheaper, but also make the manufacturing of personalised products profitable. Mass-made-to-measure, adjusting existing blocks of garments to people's measurements, is already leading the way into the future. Tomorrow, we will have fully automated semi-personalised garments made by machines. As a result, production will be possible again in high-wage countries – which becomes even more attractive in the context of future pandemic threats. The new fast fashion will be automated, local and individualised – and much less harmful for the environment.

N°7

NAVIGATING THE INTELLIGENT ENVIRONMENT

GARMENTS AS CONTROLLER

In recent years, the number of digital tools we use in our daily lives has steadily increased. Cell phones and tabloids have been accompanied by a number of apps and wearables to shop, communicate and control our health. With the functionalisation of garments, all these devices will be consolidated in one: clothes. In the context of an increasingly intelligent environment, garments will not only replace existing tools, but also control the smart objects that surround us: from opening doors, to switching on the smart lighting system, to parking our self-driving car. Moreover, they will identify us with the help of personalised sewn-in sensors, which facilitates travelling or paying bills. As a result, clothes will become our assistants, who we will assign with various tasks to make our lives easier.

CONCLUSION

SUITS FOR EARTH

"Clothes make the man. Naked people have little or no influence on society." What Mark Twain observed in the late 19th century might be more true in the future than ever. The meaning, however, seems to be shifting. Whereas in times of fading dress codes and blurring class distinctions a person's impact on society will depend less on the elegance and formality of their appearance, instead clothing's power to express individuality and personal convictions is likely to increase. Moreover, the promise of smart clothes checking our heartbeat or pay our bills, puts this quote into a new light. Garments might one day really "make" the man – by controlling and protecting our health and mastering our daily life.

Most importantly, however, clothes will not only remain as important as in Twain's days, they will gain in importance, for the individual and society as a whole. One reason is an obvious yet rarely thought of one: With the continuous growth of the world's population more clothes will be needed. By 2050, almost 10 billion people are expected to live on our planet,[28] and they will want to be dressed.

The other reasons for the increasing importance of clothing centre around the shifting needs of a changing society. An ageing population and unhealthy lifestyles will lead to a massive increase in chronic illnesses that will have to be dealt with in everyday life. Also, the risk of pandemics will remain a steady component of urban life. Clothes, as our second skin, will play a vital role in handling these tasks. Moreover, ongoing individualisation will fuel the expectations of a personalised environment, from what we eat to what we wear. As digitalisation moves on, the development of interlinked private and professional environments will call for simple ways and tools to be navigated. And climate change will subject even regions with temperate climates to extreme weather conditions. Clothes, as our daily companions, could help us to master these various challenges.

For the first time in history, technological progress is promising to expand the traditional functions of clothing, protection from harsh weather on the one hand and social representation on the other, towards an active interaction with the digital infrastructure and enhancement of our natural capabilities to obtain better health and performance.

But where does this lead us? Will we witness total disruption in clothing and actually build suits suitable for our journey to Mars? To answer these questions and to get a realistic idea of the future of clothing, it is necessary to assess the new potentials in a broader context based on two questions: Are the changes technically possible? And what are the long-term benefits for the wearers and for society?

Disruption is a common theme in many sectors from banking to mobility. But even though we are witnessing a fundamental transformation in the shift from analogue to digital media, the actual speed of change is in many cases slower than often assumed, especially when it comes to the hardware of our everyday life. Despite the many changes, there is much continuity in the clothing sector. There are various technological obstacles to make clothes interconnected and comfortable or even aesthetically pleasing. Time to have a concluding, critical look at the main future functions of clothing and evaluate their chances and limitations.

PROTECTION: Whereas protection has always been clothing's primary function, this old task has the potential to reach a next level in the future. In context of an aging society and changing environmental conditions, such as longer periods of heat and drought, air pollution and smog, as well as the rise of chronic illness and pandemics, more elaborate and different types of protection will be required. The products on the market today range from bikinis that sense when our skin is about to get sunburn, to virus-resistant jackets[29] and special clothing for the elderly with extra resistant material on arms and legs to prevent their fragile skin from tearing.[30] In the future, protective clothing is likely to borrow from the innovation in military and extreme sports, such as suits with integrated temperature regulation, which could one day protect elderly and ill people from the risks of extreme temperatures. Moreover, it is likely that clothing could play a vital role in protecting us from future pandemics, for example by integrating sensors that remind us to maintain social distance or warn us to avoid contagious areas. At the far end of the spectrum is the prototype of a vest to protect vital human tissue, particularly stem cells, from being devastated by solar radiation in deep space or on any possible future missions to Mars.[31] Comparable mechanisms are being produced to shield us from harmful gamma radiation in the case of a future radiological accident or attack. Whereas protection from the elements will remain the main function of clothing, more sophisticated and new forms of protection from environmental and everyday life risks are likely to play a vital role for health risk groups and for geographical regions suffering the worst effects of climate change.

SOCIAL REPRESENTATION: The representation of social belonging is the other traditional function of clothing next to protection. As dress codes have become less binding and casualisation has steadily substituted the suit and tie from most work places, the representation of personality to others has gained in importance. In the future, automated customisation and the facilitation of personalised fashion with virtual design, paired with the customers' growing wish for more individuality, are likely to promote this development. DIY apps for home use and walk-in stores offering the 3D printing of their customers' own sketches are even promising a future of entirely self-made or semi-self-made clothes. The limitations of this trend will, on the one hand, be the technological feasibility. So far, 3D printers are still restricted to high-end fashion and art, as the production is time-intensive and costly, and DIY design will remain complicated and laborious for non-professionals to use. On the other hand, the expression of individuality will be likely to reach its limits independently of the technological obstacles. Despite fading dress codes, consumer behaviour is still rather uniform; people, maybe also in the future, prefer not to stand out in the crowd. In the context of the continuing fragmentation of society and the resultant social isolation of many, this tendency might even increase; the value of community is likely to be rediscovered and with it the usefulness of dress codes to express social belonging. In addition, the growing complexity of everyday life might lead to a wish for more simplicity and less decision making, especially when it comes to basic needs such as clothes and food, which would likewise favour a less colourful but more homogenous future. Whereas some will embrace the full potential of the new ways to represent personality, others, probably a majority, will swim with the current; their clothes again marking the belonging to their culture and society.

INTERACTION: For the first time garments have the potential to interact with their environment. Rather than passively accompanying us through our lives, clothes could become active in helping us with everyday life tasks and the navigation of our connected environment. Scientists and experts from the field of material science and technology are working together to make garments "smart" for that purpose. Their long-term vision is that the jacket controlling the phone when we ride a bike will one day substitute that phone entirely; that the various tools to steer the internet of things could be fused in one: clothing. In addition, garments are supposed to become like a second self, a means to identify oneself to others and to our intelligent environment in order to safely shop online, pay bills or automatically open doors with a touch of the sleeve. The latest progress in the miniaturisation of sensors and material sciences speaks in favour of the feasibility of this goal, as one day sensors could be interwoven into any type of material. The benefits of consolidating a multitude of digital tools into one, wearable remote control conducting our intelligent environment is also evident. At the same time, the fusion of technology and clothing is still in its early stages and years will pass until the interconnection of garments is truly invisible. Moreover, the further dependency on technology will be considered a downside by many consumers, and for good reason. To have one tool managing our private life carries various risks, such as the hacking of door locks, computers and the theft of personal data. For the same reasons, the smart environment itself, often regarded as a given component of tomorrow's world, could partly remain science fiction and with it the textile remote control. If bill paying clothes will become a reality one day, they are likely to appeal to tech-savvy customers to command their even more highly connected home.

ENHANCEMENT: The main purpose of clothing has always been to protect the wearer from the outside, from heat, cold and wet weather. Now clothes have the potential to no longer only protect what they are shielding but to improve it – to enhance our health, performance and looks. The spectrum of enhancing clothes in sports today ranges from smart yoga pants instructing the wearer how to do the exercises to running shoes analysing the way the foot hits the concrete. The health sector's focus of innovation includes the development of textiles to check the wearer's heartbeat or blood pressure, integrated pedometers to fight obesity and drug releasing textiles. The latter is also a target of the beauty industry, which is investing in research on textiles releasing anti-aging ingredients. Currently, robotics engineers are working on the development of various wearable robots, such as overalls with built in power, that automatically stimulate people's muscles through contractions in order to boost their strength.[32] Like a soft exoskeleton to be worn under everyday clothing, the wearer's performance in sports and any kind of physical work could be improved. Even though enhancement clearly is a goal in our performance-based society, the limits are those of any other type of functional clothing: technological feasibility, affordability and people's fear of further dependence on technology. However, enhancing functional clothes will certainly find market opportunity in extreme sports, the military and in specific health areas, mainly for the purpose to improve the health and everyday life of the elderly and the chronically ill.

Looking at the enormous potential of clothing to improve and expand its functions, it becomes clear that, while some possibilities will be true innovations with a clear benefit for a majority, others will either never pass the reality test or build small niche markets for specific interest groups. It is possible that we will never create suits that will allow us to walk on Mars. But even if we will, their importance for the future of clothing is limited. What we really need are suits (and other clothes) for Earth. The real mission to Mars is not to leave behind a broken planet and resettle in new territories, but to make the Earth a good place to live in the 22nd century and beyond.

For the clothing industry this means primarily to start tackling the enormous task of dressing 10 billion people while reversing its position as one of the most polluting industries globally.

The progress in the automation of the production and the virtualisation of design will certainly do their parts to fulfil this mission. Whereas sewing robots still have to prove their practicability, the number of jobs carried out by machines is steadily growing, which makes production cheaper and clothes more affordable. Likewise, digital design is not only speeding up the design process, it also helps to reduce textile waste as sample-making is no longer necessary. Simultaneously, the research on new artificial materials to reduce the depletion of natural resources as well as the rediscovery of more sustainable natural fibres is paving the way towards a smaller ecological footprint. Moreover, growing transparency in the digital age will shed more light on unsustainable business practices, even in the most distant places of the planet.

However, as with any technological progress, the adaptation in society takes time and needs to be carefully planned in advance. The changes in the production of clothing, mainly the automation of an increasing number of tasks traditionally carried out by humans, will lead to a massive loss of jobs. It is vital to consider now other job opportunities for these people and organise the necessary education in different, maybe more elaborate skills in the clothing sector. Technological innovation requires social innovation. The development of tomorrow's clothes needs to be based on an understanding of where and how garments will serve us best. The future of clothing affects the future of our society, our culture, work and everyday life. It starts now.

APPENDIX

THE FUTURE OF FASHION AS SEEN BY JOHN M. ARMLEDER

Scabal asked: What Is the Future of Fashion? John Armleder (see page 167) answered something like this: It's all to be found in a sphere and a gold pattern on violet wallpaper. To be concrete: Armleder's proposal for the future of fashion is a sphere made of brass with a diameter of 50 cm and a wallpaper in mother-of-pearl violet sporting a mesmerizing regular pattern of three globe-like objects. In combination these two artworks could well be imagined in a chic creative household, an avantgarde discothèque or an airport lounge. There is something touchingly glamorous about the shine of the brass and the sparkle of the gold print on the wallpaper held in violet, a colour that particularly in fashion is known as perhaps difficult to combine, and gaudy in monochrome format. Only absolute masters of style can bring this colour combination to new heights.

How exactly do these artefacts represent the future of fashion? It is part of Armleder's artistic practice to work with a library of graphic codes, as representative of the world of today. It is a way to decode the complexity of life and make it simpler, easier, more accessible. Why wallpaper? It allows a regular repetition of shapes, forming a pattern and patterns have an effect on our brain: the singular shape loses its meaning and becomes something entirely new. The spheres and globes come to us with a futuristic message, at once entertaining and scientific, looking like disco balls as much as cells in the human body.

John's statement on the future of fashion is an intervention as much as a structuralist study on pattern recognition. The enigmatic cool it atomises is a reference for the incomprehensible popular attraction of fashion today. Art and fashion are both an escape from the normality and profanity of everyday life. Fashion and art are part of everything today and can be found everywhere – there is no longer a context required. However, it is also true that fashion is just clothes and art is everything.

John Armleder, Juste Debout, 2019, Bronze, Diameter: 50 cm

In the same way Armleder changes our ideas of what the format of an exhibition can be he challenges the old idea of the grand artistic gesture. Armleder's work with appropriation and references is incredibly liberating on different levels for everybody who chooses to engage. On an intellectual level, due to the cues of art history and the play with traditional signifiers and, on an emotional level, due to the lighthearted spirit of every work, every installation and every exhibition.

Concerning fashion, Armleder now plans to create a fabric sporting the globe pattern and produce lining for suits, ties and pochettes for your suit jacket. The future is now.

John Armleder, Workshop, 2019, Screenprinted wallpaper.

JOHN M. ARMLEDER

John M. Armleder was born in 1948 in Geneva, where he lives and works today. In the 1960s he studied fine art at the Ecole des Beaux-Arts in Geneva and the Glamorgan Summer School in Britain. Later he co-founded the Ecart Group, which was closely linked to Fluxus, the international and interdisciplinary movement which rated the artistic process higher than the finished object and played an important role in introducing artists such as Joseph Beuys and Andy Warhol to a wider audience. Armleder is known for an everchanging body of work which includes performance, sculpture, design, drawing, painting, sound and curatorial projects. John M. Armleder is regarded as one of the most important conceptual artists of today. His works are included in collections all over the world, including The MoMA Museum of Modern Art in New York, the MAMCO Museum of Modern and Contemporary Art in Geneva, the Kunstmuseum Basel, the Rubell Family Collection in Miami, and many others. He has held professorships at the Braunschweiger Hochschule für Bildende Künste and the Ecole Cantonale d'Art de Lausanne.

SIMONE ACHERMANN

MA EUROPEAN CULTURE UCL, CO-FOUNDER OF W.I.R.E.
AND EDITOR-IN-CHIEF OF ABSTRAKT

Simone Achermann engages with developments and trends in society, business and cultural sciences and is responsible for the ABSTRAKT book series (NZZ Verlag). She is the author and editor of a variety of publications, including "Mind the Future – compendium for contemporary trends" and the Suhrkamp series "What counts". Before taking up her role at W.I.R.E. she worked for several years as a communications consultant, focusing on the area of corporate social responsibility and writing texts and speeches for top managers in business and social fields. Simone Achermann studied cultural sciences at University College London.

STEPHAN SIGRIST

DR. SC. ETH ZÜRICH, FOUNDER AND
HEAD OF THINK TANK W.I.R.E.

The founder and head of the W.I.R.E. think tank has spent many years analysing interdisciplinary developments in business and society, focusing on the implications of digitisation in the life sciences, financial services, media, infrastructure and mobility. He is the publisher of the ABSTRAKT book series, author of a number of publications and a keynote speaker at international conferences. With W.I.R.E., he advises decision makers on the development of long-term strategies and innovation projects, and supports companies in the redesign of future-oriented spaces for employees and the exchange with clients. After studying biochemistry at the ETH Zurich, he initially joined Hoffman-La Roche's medical research team. He subsequently went on to work at Roland Berger Strategy Consultants as a management consultant and at the Gottlieb Duttweiler Institute.

W.I.R.E.

W.I.R.E. is one of the leading interdisciplinary think tanks. In more than 10 years of engaging with global trends in business, science and society, the Swiss idea laboratory has focused on identifying new trends early and translating them into strategies and areas for action by private companies and public institutions. At the interface between academia and practical application, W.I.R.E.'s critical mindset and political neutrality mark it as distinctive. Its key topics are the digital economy, social innovation and future-proofing. The think tank places its expertise at the service of the general public, private enterprise and public agencies, in fields ranging from life science, financial services and media to food and industry.

W.I.R.E.'s document- and experience-based knowledge transfer formats are notable for their harmony of form and content, and the outstanding quality of their aesthetics and design. The think tank boasts an international network of experts, thought leaders and decision makers.

thewire.ch

SCABAL

Founded in 1938, Scabal is the world's foremost producer of luxury fabrics, supplying elite tailors and fashion houses. Scabal also crafts its own label suits, jackets and shirts in made-to-measure and prêt-à-porter, while Scabal stores that carry the apparel and accessories can be found in key cities across Europe and Asia. Today Scabal is still family-owned and its heritage mill in England has been weaving since 1899. The brand also offers full European production in both cloth and clothing, using only the best raw materials sourced directly from suppliers, so from sheep to shop, field to fold, and camel to coat, Scabal can always ensure the highest quality.

scabal.com

BOOKS

Breward C. (2003), *Fashion*, Oxford: Oxford University Press.

Breward C. (2016), *The Suit: Form, Function and Style*, London: Reaktion Books.

English B. (2013), *A Cultural History of Fashion in the 20th and 21st Centuries*, New York: Bloomsbury.

Farley Gordon J. & Hill C. (2014), *Sustainable Fashion: Past, Present and Future*, New York: Bloomsbury Academic.

Fletcher K. & Grose L. (2012), *Fashion & Sustainability: Design for Change*, London: Laurence King Publishing (reprint).

Fletcher K. & Tham M. (2016), *Routledge Handbook for Sustainability and Fashion*, Abingdon: Routledge.

Gwilt A. (2015), *Fashion Design for Living*, Abingdon: Routledge.

Harari Y. (2011), *Sapiens: A biref history of humankind*, New York: Vintage.

Harari Y. (2017), *Homo Deus: A brief history of tomorrow*, New York: Vintage.

Minney S. (2016), *Slow Fashion: Aesthetics Meets Ethics*, Oxford: New Internationalist.

Sennett R. (2009), *The Craftsman*, London: Penguin.

Von Busch O. (2018), *Vital Vogue: A biosocial perspective on fashion*, New York: SelfPassage.

Wood J. (2007), *Design for Micro-Utopias: Making the Unthinkable Possible*, Farnham: Ashgate Publishing Limited.

DISSERTATIONS

Tham M. (2008), 'Lucky People Forecast: a systemic futures perspective on fashion and sustainability', doctoral thesis, Goldsmiths, University of London, London.

FILM, TELEVISION AND RADIO

A Stitch in Time (2008), [TV programme] BBC FOUR.

JOURNAL ARTICLES

Hsu, P. C., Liu, X., Liu, C., Xie, X., Lee, H. R., Welch, A. J. & Cui, Y. (2014). 'Personal thermal management by metallic nanowire-coated textile', *Nano letters*, 15(1), 365-371.

Singh, A. and Nijhar, K. (2018), 'Recent developments in the garment supply chain', *Automation in Garment Manufacturing* (377-396). Woodhead Publishing.

Wu, Y., Shah, D. U., Liu, C., Yu, Z., Liu, J., Ren, X. & Scherman, O. A. (2017), 'Bioinspired supramolecular fibers drawn from a multiphase self-assembled hydrogel', *Proceedings of the National Academy of Sciences*, 114(31), 8163-8168.

ONLINE RESOURCES

Arthur R. (2015), '5 THINGS YOUR CLOTHES WILL BE ABLE TO DO IN THE FUTURE' *Fashionista* Available online: https://fashionista.com/2015/09/clothes-of-the-future [Accessed 6 Dec. 2019].

Bauck W. (2017), 'How technology is shaping the future of sustainable fashion' *Fashionista*, Available online: fashionista.com/2017/10/fashion-design-technology-sustainable-textiles-2017 [Accessed 6 Dec. 2019].
Bridghtside (n.d.), '16 Amazing Items of Clothing We Will Wear in the Future'. *Bridghtside*, Available online: https://brightside.me/wonder-curiosities/16-amazing-items-of-clothing-we-will-wear-in-the-future-415660/ [Accessed 6 Dec. 2019].

Brownlee J. (2015), 'Would You Don These Sci-Fi Skin Suits If They Could Improve Your Health?.' *Fast Company*, Available online: https://www.fastcompany.com/3045962/would-you-wear-these-sci-fi-skin-suits-if-they-could-improve-your-health [Accessed 6 Dec. 2019].

Budds D. (2016), 'This Designer Is Making Brand-Name Fashion Friendlier To Kids With Disabilities.' *Fast Company*, Available online: fastcompany.com/3056989/meet-the-designer-making-brand-name-fashion-friendlier-to-kids-to-kids-with-disabilities [Accessed 6 Dec. 2019].

Carrasco Rozas A. (2017), 'Sustainable Textile Innovations: Coffee Ground Fibre.' *Fashion United*, Available online: https://

fashionunited.uk/news/fashion/sustainable-textile-innovations-coffee-ground-fibre/2017061624856 [Accessed 6 Dec. 2019].

Electroloom (2016), 'Electroloom - The World's First 3D Fabric Printer.' *Kickstarter*, Available online: kickstarter.com/projects/electroloom/electroloom-the-worlds-first-3d-fabric-printer [Accessed 6 Dec. 2019].

fashion2apparel (2018), 'Automation in Apparel Manufacturing Industry.' *fashion2apparel*, Available online: https://fashion2apparel.blogspot.com/2018/03/automation-apparel-manufacturing.html [Accessed 6 Dec. 2019].

fibre2fashion.com (n.d.), 'B2B Marketplace, B2B Business Solutions, Business Directory.' *fibre2fashion*, Available online: https://www.fibre2fashion.com/ [Accessed 6 Dec. 2019].

fibre2fashion.com (2012), 'Legacy of the celestial flower: lotus fibre fabrics,' *fibre2fashion*, Available online: fibre2fashion.com/industry-article/6589/legacy-of-the-celestial-flower-lotus-fibre-fabrics [Accessed 6 Dec. 2019].

Gadis R. (2014), 'What Is The Future Of Fabric? These Smart Textiles Will Blow Your Mind.' *Forbes*, Available online: https://www.forbes.com/sites/forbesstylefile/2014/05/07/what-is-the-future-of-fabric-these-smart-textiles-will-blow-your-mind/#45a0ce48599b [Accessed 6 Dec. 2019].

Google (n.d.), 'JACQUARD,' *Google*, Available online: atap.google.com/jacquard/ [Accessed 6 Dec. 2019].

Izzy Camilleri (2016), 'IZ Collection Fall/Winter 2016.' *Izzy Camilleri*, Available online: http://www.izzycamilleri.com/galleries/iz-collection/ [Accessed 6 Dec. 2019].

Leach A. (2017), 'In the Future We Won't Own Clothes, We'll Rent Them.' *Highsnobiety*, Available online: highsnobiety.com/2017/08/02/circular-economy-fashion/ [Accessed 6 Dec. 2019].

Lee T. (2017), The 'digital handmade': how 3D printing became a new craft technology.' *The Conversation*, Available online: http://theconversation.com/the-digital-handmade-how-3d-printing-became-a-new-craft-technology-77559 [Accessed 6 Dec. 2019].

Lunn O. (2017), 'A brief history of fashion designers imagining the clothes of the future.' *I-D Vice*, Available online: https://i-d.vice.com/en_us article/8xgqax/a-brief-history-of-fashion-designers-imagining-the-clothes-of-the-future [Accessed 6 Dec. 2019].

Mintel Press Team (2012), 'Comfort meets style as casualisation takes hold of the US men's clothing market.' *Mintel*, Available online: https://www.mintel.com/press-centre/retail-press-centre/comfort-meets-style-as-casualization-takes-hold-of-the-us-mens-clothing-market [Accessed 6 Dec. 2019].

New Cloth Market (2008), 'Future Scenario, Future of Clothing, Clothes Trend Forecasting.' *fibre2fashion*, Available online: https://www.fibre2fashion.com/industry-article/3455/the-future-of-clothing [Accessed 6 Dec. 2019].

Nguyen H. (2018), 'The future of clothing could be both fashionable and functional.' *YouGov*, Available online: https://today.yougov.com/topics/sports/articles-reports/2018/02/27/future-clothing-could-be-both-fashionable-and-func [Accessed 6 Dec. 2019].

Pennsylvania State University (2016), 'Self-healing textiles not only repair themselves, but can neutralize chemicals.' *Phys.Org*, Available online: phys.org/news/2016-07-self-healing-textiles-neutralize-chemicals.html [Accessed 6 Dec. 2019].

Perry P. (2016), 'Future Clothes Will Turn Us into Living Art.' *Big Think*, Available online: https://bigthink.com/philip-perry/future-clothes-will-turn-us-into-living-art [Accessed 6 Dec. 2019].

Peters A. (2016), '5 New Solutions For The Fashion Industry's Sustainability Problem.' *Fast Company*, Available online: https://www.fastcompany.com/3055925/5-new-solutions-for-the-fashion-industrys-sustainability-problem [Accessed 6 Dec. 2019].

Petter O. (2017), '*IS GENDER-NEUTRAL CLOTHING THE FUTURE OF FASHION?*' *Independent*, Available online: independent.co.uk/life-style/fashion/gender-neutral-clothing-fashion-future-male-female-women-wildfang-hm-a8017446.html [Accessed 6 Dec. 2019].

Petter O. (2017), '*JOHN LEWIS GENDER NEUTRAL CLOTHING LABELS FACES PUBLIC BACKLASH.*' *Independent*, Available online: https://www.independent.co.uk/life-style/fashion/john-lewis-gender-neutral-clothing-labels-response-sex-boys-girls-men-women-a7928006.html [Accessed 6 Dec. 2019].

PRNewswire (2015), 'Conductive Materials For Smart Textiles Market 2017.' *PRNewswire*, Available online: https://www.prnewswire.com/news-releases/conductive-materials-for-smart-textiles-market-2017-300540494.html [Accessed 6 Dec. 2019].

PulpWorks (n.d.), 'PulpWorks: Molding a better world.' Available online: http://www.pulpworksinc.com [Accessed 6 Dec. 2019].

Segran E. (2017), 'Can fast fashion be ethical? Reformation is rewriting the rules.' *Fast Company*, Available online: fastcompany.com/3067776/can-fast-fashion-be-ethical-sustainable-reformation-is-rewriting-the-rules [Accessed 6 Dec. 2019].

Segran E. (2017), 'Fashion's Future May Rest On An Old Technology: Glue', *Fast Company*, Available online: https://www.fastcompany.com/40465659/how-glue-may-speed-up-the-coming-robot-revolution-in-clothes-making [Accessed 6 Dec. 2019].

Sewbo (n.d.), 'Sewbo Home.' *Sewbo*, Available online: http://www.sewbo.com/ [Accessed 6 Dec. 2019].

Sharklet (n.d.), 'Sharklet Home.' *Sharklet*, Available online: https://www.sharklet.com [Accessed 6 Dec. 2019].

Softwear Automation (n.d.), 'Home - Softwear Automation' *Softwear Automation*, Available online: http://softwearautomation.com/ [Accessed 6 Dec. 2019].

Sonofatailor.com (n.d.), 'Son of a Tailor - Custom Fitted T-Shirts.' *Son of a Tailor*, Available online: https://www.sonofatailor.com [Accessed 6 Dec. 2019].

Sorrel C. (2015), 'An Alternative to Fast Fashion: Laser-Cut Clothing You Download And Assemble Yourself.' *Fast Company*, Available online: fastcompany.com/3053321/an-alternative-to-fast-fashion-laser-cut-clothing-you-download-and-assemble-yourself [Accessed 6 Dec. 2019].

Spinali Design (n.d.), 'Spinali Design – Classical Neviano.' *Spinali Design*, Available online: https://www.spinali-design.com/pages/classical-neviano [Accessed 6 Dec. 2019].

Tangible Media Group (2015), 'bioLogic.' *Tangible Media Group*, Available online: tangible.media.mit.edu/project/biologic/ [Accessed 6 Dec. 2019].

Taraska J. (2015), 'Programmable Clothes Are Going Commercial.' *Fast Company*, Available online: https://www.fastcompany.com/3048737/programmable-clothes-are-going-commercial?utm_source=postup&utm_medium=email&utm_campaign=wears&position=3&partner=newsletter&campaign_date=05132019 [Accessed 6 Dec. 2019].

The Associated Press (2017), '5 Reasons Why Amazon Is Experimenting With Physical Stores.' *Fortune*, Available online: https://fortune.com/2017/04/28/5-reasons-amazon-physical-stores/ [Accessed 6 Dec. 2019].

Vincent J. (2018), 'Fashion startup stops using AI tailor after it fails to size up customers correctly.' *The Verge*, Available online: https://www.theverge.com/2018/2/6/16977834/ai-fashion-fitting-original-stitch-machine-vision [Accessed 6 Dec. 2019].

WearableX (2018), 'Nadi X - Smart Yoga Pants that Guide Your Form.' *Kickstarter*, Available online: https://www.kickstarter.com/projects/1727484594/nadi-x-yoga-pants-smart-yoga-pants-for-travel-and?lang=es [Accessed 6 Dec. 2019].

Wendlandt A. (2013), 'Small labels lure big bucks in fashion's latest trend.' *Reuters*, Available online: https://www.reuters.com/article/us-fashion-investment/small-labels-lure-big-bucks-in-fashions-latest-trend-idUSBRE92C0AV20130313 [Accessed 6 Dec. 2019].

Wildfang (n.d.), 'Wildfang - Home.' *Wildfang*, Available online: https://www.wildfang.com [Accessed 6 Dec. 2019].

3D-A-Porter (n.d.), '3D VIRTUAL FITTING ROOM.' *3D-A-Porter*, Available online: http://3d-a-porter.com/services/3d-virtual-fitting-room/ [Accessed 6 Dec. 2019].

REFERENCES

INTRODUCTION

1 https://rcmtm.en.ec21.com

2 https://www.vollebak.com

3 https://www.bonbouton.com/smart-insole

TOWARDS AUTOMATION, SUSTAINABILITY AND INDIVIDUALITY

DRIVERS OF CHANGE

SUSTAINABILITY

4 BOF Team (2018), 'Fashion in 2018 / 08. Sustainability Credibility', *Business of Fashion*, Available online: https://www.businessoffashion.com/articles/intelligence/top-industry-trends-2018-8-sustainability-credibility [Accessed 6 Dec. 2019].

5 A blockchain is a digital ledger, consisting of a growing list of data recrods called blocks, which are linked using cryptography. Each block contains a cryptographic hash of the previous block, a timestamp and transaction data. Originally used for cryptocurrencies, blockchain solutions in the clothing industry are based on its ability to create a physical-digital link between goods and their digital identities on a blockchain. Often, a cryptographic seal or serial number acts as the physical identifier, linking back to the individual product's "digital twin".

Radocchia S. (2018), 'Altering The Apparel Industry: How The Blockchain Is Changing Fashion', *Forbes*, Available online: https://www.forbes.com/sites/samantharadocchia/2018/06/27/altering-the-apparel-industry-how-the-blockchain-is-changing-fashion/ [Accessed 6 Dec. 2019].

BLURRING GENDER ROLES

6 Radin S. (2018), 'THESE GENDER-NEUTRAL LABELS TO WATCH PROVIDE INCLUSIVE COMMUNITIES THROUGH CLOTHES', *Fashionista*, Available online: https://fashionista.com/2018/05/unisex-non-binary-gender-neutral-clothing-brands-2018 [Accessed 6 Dec. 2019].

7 Saner E. (2017), 'Joy of unisex: the rise of gender-neutral clothing', *The Guardian*, Available online: https://www.theguardian.com/lifeandstyle/2017/sep/04/joy-unisex-gender-neutral-clothing-john-lewis [Accessed 6 Dec. 2019].

INDIVIDUALISATION AND FADING FORMALITY

8 Mintel Press Team (2012), 'Comfort meets style as casualisation takes hold of the US men's clothing market', *Mintel*, Available online: https://www.mintel.com/press-centre/retail-press-centre/comfort-meets-style-as-casualization-takes-hold-of-the-us-mens-clothing-market [Accessed 6 Dec. 2019].

FUNCTIONALISATION

9 WearableX (2018), 'Nadi X - Smart Yoga Pants that Guide Your Form', *Kickstarter*, Available online: https://www.kickstarter.com/projects/1727484594/nadi-x-yoga-pants-smart-yoga-pants-for-travel-and?lang=es [Accessed 6 Dec. 2019].

10 Spinali Design (n.d.), 'Spinali Design – Classical Neviano', *Spinali Design*, Available online: https://www.spinali-design.com/pages/classical-neviano [Accessed 6 Dec. 2019].

11 Google (n.d.), 'JACQUARD', *Google*, Available online: atap.google.com/jacquard/ [Accessed 6 Dec. 2019].

12 Hodson H. (2016), 'Smart clothes adapt so you are always the right temperature', *NewScientist*, Available online: https://www.newscientist.com/article/2074964-smart-clothes-adapt-so-you-are-always-the-right-temperature/ [Accessed 6 Dec. 2019].

13 Lewis O. & Harash R. (2017), 'Mars astronaut radiation shield set for moon mission trial: Developer', *Reuters*, Available online: https://www.reuters.com/article/us-spacex-mars-israel/mars-astronaut-radiation-shield-set-for-moon-mission-trial-developer-idUSKBN16A0ZJ [Accessed 6 Dec. 2019].

StemRad (n.d.), 'StemRad – Home', *StemRad*, Available online: https://stemrad.com [Accessed 6 Dec. 2019].

VIRTUALISATION

14 Moore M. (2018), 'UBS Digitally Cloned Its Chief Economist So He Wouldn't Miss His Meetings', *Fortune*, Available online https://fortune.com/2018/07/05/ubs-digital-clone-chief-economist-daniel-kalt/ [Accessed 6 Dec. 2019].

DEMOCRATISATION OFPRODUCTION

15 Electroloom (2016), 'Electroloom - The World's First 3D Fabric Printer', *Kickstarter*, Available online: kickstarter.com/projects/electroloom/electroloom-the-worlds-first-3d-fabric-printer [Accessed 6 Dec. 2019].

16 Original Stitch (n.d.), 'Original Stitch - Story', *Original Stitch*, Available online: https://shop.originalstitch.com/pages/about-us?ls=en [Accessed 6 Dec. 2019].

17 Wendlandt A. (2013), 'Small labels lure big bucks in fashion's latest trend', *Reuters*, Available online: https://www.reuters.com/article/us-fashion-investment/small-labels-lure-big-bucks-in-fashions-latest-trend-idUSBRE92C0AV20130313 [Accessed 6 Dec. 2019].

CASES

18 American Cleaning Institute (n.d.), 'Saving Water', *American Cleaning Institute*, Available online: https://www.cleaninginstitute.org/sustainable-cleaning/saving-water [Accessed 6 Dec. 2019].

19 Electrolux Group (2017), 'Don't Overwash – new project drives sustainable care habits', *Electrolux Group*, Available online: https://www.electroluxgroup.com/en/dont-overwash-new-project-drives-sustainable-care-habits-23427/ [Accessed 6 Dec. 2019].

20 Fashion Revolution (2016), 'Don't Overwash: it's time to change the way we care', *Fashion Revolution*, Available online: fashionrevolution.org/dont-overwash-its-time-to-change-the-way-we-care/ [Accessed 6 Dec. 2019].

21 Graham G. (2018), '2018 was the year AI influencers and digital models took over fashion', *Dazed Digital*, Available online: https://www.dazeddigital.com/fashion/article/42484/1/cgi-models-ai-influencers-lil-miquela-digital-models-trend-shudu-noonoouri [Accessed 6 Dec. 2019].

22 Pàmies P. & Stoddart A. (2013), 'Materials for drug delivery', *Nature Materials* (12), 957.

23 Pàmies P. & Stoddart A. (2013), 'Materials for drug delivery', *Nature Materials* (12), 957.

24 Van Elven M. (2018), 'People do not wear at least 50 percent of their wardrobes, says study', *Fashion United*, Available online: https://fashionunited.uk/news/fashion/people-do-not-wear-at-least-50-percent-of-their-wardrobes-according-to-study/2018081638356 [Accessed 6 Dec. 2019].

25 Inside Out Style (n.d.), 'Imogen Lamport's Inside Out Style – Easy Style Solutions for Every Woman', *Inside Out Style*, Available online: https://insideoutstyleblog.com [Accessed 6 Dec. 2019].

26 Clothes Doctor (n.d.), 'Clothes Doctor', *Clothes Doctor*, Available online: https://clothes-doctor.com [Accessed 6 Dec. 2019].

27 https://www.shopify.com/enterprise/ecommerce-fashion-industry

CONCLUSION

28 https://www.nationalgeographic.com/news/2015/07/world-population-expected-to-reach-9-7-billion-by-2050/

29 https://www.vollebak.com/product/full-metal-jacket-black-edition/

30 https://www.buckandbuck.com/adaptive-clothing-guide/protective-clothing.html

31 https://stemrad.com

32 https://www.myseismic.com